THE 8 KEYS OF EXCELLENCE

Principles to Live By

Bobbi DePorter

Learning Forum Publications
Oceanside, California USA

Published by Learning Forum Publications

Copyright © 2000 by Bobbi DePorter. Revised 2010.

Submit all requests for reprinting to:

Learning Forum Publications
1938 Avenida del Oro
Oceanside, CA 92056
(760) 722 0072

Graphic Design: Kelley Thomas
Illustration: Ellen Duris

ISBN: 0-945525-28-1

Printed in the United States of America

*Dedicated to all the very special
Quantum Learning Network staff
who have contributed so much
over the years .*

*I acknowledge Shelby Reeder for
her contribution in the writing of*
The 8 Keys of Excellence.
*Her support of Quantum Learning Network
and understanding of our Keys,
led to finally completing a book
we have dreamed of for many years.*

*Thank you to those who
contributed stories, knowing that
we share a commitment to living
a life based on principles.*

*Most stories are in contributors' own words –
others are collaborations and interviews.*

Table of Contents

Key 4: This Is It!   83

Key 5: Commitment   111

Key 6: Ownership   147

Introduction
The 8 Keys of Excellence

*He who merely knows right principles is
not equal to him who loves them.* —Confucius

Principles are the rules that guide human behavior. Concepts like fairness, integrity, and truth are generally accepted and shared by all people. They are not tied to time or culture or history – they are objective, not subjective.

Principles define the culture of any group – family, school, club, company. They lay the groundwork for personal excellence and align groups on agreed behavior. People who are aware of their shared principles and uphold them know what to expect from one another. They experience a higher level of trust, more teamwork, and ultimately, greater success.

If you have ever belonged to a group that shared your principles, you may have noticed the feeling of teamwork, the spirit of the group, and the way all members pulled together to achieve a common goal. Shared principles create this type of environment. Working together, people are more fulfilled, willing to learn and do, and enthusiastic about things to come. In such a culture, excellence thrives and success is a natural outcome.

With this in mind, we developed the 8 Keys of Excellence many years ago by studying people who had achieved great success while maintaining personal *excellence*. We identified the traits and principles they shared and those that came up most often became our 8 Keys. They include generally accepted concepts like integrity, commitment, and responsibility.

8 Keys of Excellence

INTEGRITY
Match behavior with values
Demonstrate your positive personal values in all you do and say. Be sincere and real.

FAILURE LEADS TO SUCCESS
Learn from mistakes
View failures as feedback that provides you with the information you need to learn, grow, and succeed.

SPEAK WITH GOOD PURPOSE
Speak honestly and kindly
Think before you speak. Make sure your intention is positive and your words are sincere.

THIS IS IT!
Make the most of every moment
Focus your attention on the present moment. Keep a positive attitude.

COMMITMENT
Make your dreams happen
Take positive action. Follow your vision without wavering.

OWNERSHIP
Take responsibility for actions
Be responsible for your thoughts, feelings, words, and actions. "Own" the choices you make and the results that follow.

FLEXIBILITY
Be willing to do things differently
Recognize what's not working and be willing to change what you're doing to achieve your goal.

BALANCE
Live your best life
Be mindful of self and others while focusing on what's meaningful and important in your life. Inner happiness and fulfillment come when your mind, body, and emotions are nurtured by the choices you make.

As principles, the 8 Keys of Excellence do more than create a more positive environment – they change lives. Becoming aware of these eight principles and committing to them is both exciting and challenging, pushing us to strive for excellence and positively impacting the world we live in. For as we learn to model our beliefs, other people in our lives are influenced by our behavior and often follow the examples we set. Like falling dominoes, the process continues, each person affecting the next.

Excellence

Let's look for a moment at the meaning of excellence and its impact on our lives and on our world. Excellence is defined as *the quality of excelling, greatness, value, worth* – and when we excel we do extremely well, we shine, we stand out. Aristotle gives us a little more insight in our understanding of this powerful word ...

> *Excellence is an art won by training and habituation. We do not act rightly because we have virtue or excellence, but we rather have those because we have acted rightly. We are what we repeatedly do. Excellence, then, is not an act but a habit.* —Aristotle

In light of Aristotle's thoughts, we can consider the principles of the 8 Keys of Excellence as our guide to "act rightly" – if we make each of the 8 Keys a habit, make them part of who we are, they will lead us to excellence. If we "live" the 8 Keys of Excellence – in our homes, in our schools, in our organizations – we will truly excel!

The 8 Keys of Excellence and SuperCamp

The 8 Keys of Excellence are the foundation for SuperCamp, the academic and life-skills youth achievement summer program that we began in 1982. The program is carefully orchestrated to create a sense of belonging in an open, friendly environment and the 8 Keys are vital part of this atmosphere. They're posted on walls, modeled by staff and woven into each day's activities – the students are immersed in the 8 Keys for the duration of SuperCamp. All students agree to live by these principles while at SuperCamp, creating a feeling of community and trust. The benefits of the SuperCamp program – with the 8 Keys of Excellence at its core – have been noted worldwide. Studies show SuperCamp graduates significantly increase self-confidence and motivation, improve their grades, participate more in school, and feel measurably better about themselves.

As the relevance of the 8 Keys in the personal growth of SuperCamp students became clear we soon found that the 8 Keys were making their way into our personal lives, our family lives, and our culture at Quantum Learning Network (QLN). In addition, as the teachers of SuperCamp grads became aware of something "different" the 8 Keys of Excellence soon found a place in schools and are now successfully used in classrooms nationwide and internationally. As you can see, the 8 Keys spread easily. They encompass basic principles that most of us already know to be "right" behavior and provide a common language – a bond – that brings groups of people closer.

The 8 Keys of Excellence can be used in almost any group setting. Here are some ideas on bringing the 8 Keys into your home, your classroom, and your organization. Many of these suggestions are adaptable for other areas so check all three sections for ideas.

The 8 Keys of Excellence in Your Home

Introducing the 8 Keys in your home provides a great opportunity for meaningful and ongoing family communication that is so often lacking in our busy lives. Outlining and agreeing to live by the principles of the 8 Keys brings the family together with a common purpose – and every family member can make a significant contribution to the process.

• **Introduce the Keys:** The idea of the family "living" the 8 Keys could be introduced at a special meal or other family gathering by reading the definitions of all the Keys and sharing simple stories to illustrate them. Then everyone agrees to work together toward making the Keys part of their lives and part of the family's life.

• **It's a process:** It's important to keep the 8 Keys "alive" in your family on a daily basis. The Keys are easily understood by all age groups so everyone can take part in this ongoing process. Every night at dinner could be a good time to ask family members to share something they noticed about one of the Keys during the day – something along the lines of how they (or someone they observed) either used or forgot to use one of the Keys. Some days this could be a very quick share from each person, other days it could lead to a fun and interesting family discussion.

• **A Key for the week:** Family members can take turns choosing and introducing a new Key to focus on each week (or whatever time period your family chooses). This could be done at a special family "Key Talk" gathering on Sunday nights and, although younger children may need some help, everyone can have a turn. Be creative and make it a fun event that everyone can look forward to.

- **Model the Keys:** The first step in integrating the 8 Keys into your home is by living and modeling them yourself. One of the five Quantum Learning tenets that drives our actions at SuperCamp is "Everything Speaks," meaning that whatever you say and whatever you do sends a message. Become aware of your own behavior and do your best to uphold the Keys. If you slip, don't cover up. Instead, ask your kids, *What Key did I just violate?* – and turn the occasion into a learning experience for your family.

- **Shift their focus:** At the end of the day, instead of asking your kids *What did you do today?* ask *How did you show up today? What Key did you live?* They'll begin thinking during the day of how they'll answer your question that night.

- **Catch your kids using the Keys:** Praise them when you notice them showing Commitment or Speaking with Good Purpose. Often we focus on behavior only when a child misbehaves – the Keys give us many opportunities to recognize, acknowledge, and encourage positive behavior, and make our kids feel good about themselves.

- **Use the Keys to correct misbehavior:** Instead of labeling a child's behavior with a negative statement such as *Stop being mean to your brother,* try asking an open-ended question like *What Key is challenging you right now?* or *What Key do you need to focus on?* and help your child to come up with Speak with Good Purpose. Allowing the child to recognize, label, and correct his or her own behavior is much more powerful than the former approach!

In addition to these suggestions for making the 8 Keys of Excellence part of your family's life, there are more ideas in the following sections that you may want to adapt for use in your home.

The 8 Keys of Excellence in Your Classroom

In schools, the Keys provide a sense of purpose and commonality. Thornton Township High School south of Chicago has found that teaching the Keys has even helped diminish behavior problems. Northwood Middle School in Woodstock, Illinois, discovered a greater sense of community. The 8 Keys of Excellence are part of many schools around the world, and wherever they're introduced, students, educators, and parents find that they provide a meaningful way to improve cooperation and teamwork and create a supportive, trusting environment where each student is valued and respected and real learning can take place.

Carole Allen, an educator and past SuperCamp facilitator, has used the Keys in her classrooms for years. She has used them with both elementary and high school students with great success. As a teacher at M.E.A.D. Creative Learning Center, an alternative school for at-risk youth near Spokane, Washington, she made the Keys the foundation of her classroom and they worked so well that other teachers successfully followed her lead. Carole's goal is always to get the Keys to the "automatic level," where the students begin to "see the world through the Keys."

Here are some suggestions on how to make the Keys part of your classroom – and part of your students' lives.

- **Post the 8 Keys in a prominent place:** Make sure they're always visible – and big enough to be read easily from anywhere in the classroom. We use eight large key-shaped signs, one for each Key. You can create your own, enlist the help of your students, or order ready-made sets from QLN.

- **Introduce a new Key daily, weekly, or even monthly:** Discuss the definition. Games, activities, demonstrations, and facilitated discussions are effective ways to make the Keys memorable. Tie the Key in with daily activities.

- **Use stories and examples to explain the Keys:** Personal stories from your own life make a strong impact – and encourage your students to share stories of their own. You can also read aloud to your students from the selections in this book. Each chapter focuses on one of the 8 Keys – a short definition of the Key is followed by meaningful true stories that illustrate the essence of the Key.

- **Catch your students using the Keys:** Praise them when you notice them Speaking with Good Purpose or showing Commitment. Often, we focus on behavior only when a student misbehaves. The Keys give us an opportunity to recognize, acknowledge, and encourage positive behavior.

- **Use the Keys to correct misbehavior:** Instead of labeling a student's behavior with statements like *you're not paying attention* or *stop talking during reading time,* try directing the student's attention to the Keys. Ask open-ended questions like *What Key is challenging you right* *now?* or *What Key do you need to focus on?* With this approach the student is able to recognize, label, and correct his or her own behavior – much more powerful than the former approach!

- **Model the Keys in your own life:** If you want your students to take you seriously, you need to model the Keys yourself. Become aware of your own behavior and do your best to uphold the Keys. If you do slip, don't cover up. Instead, turn the occasion into an opportunity to teach the Keys and ask your students, *What Key did I just violate?* Let them know that you are working on living the Keys all the time, just as they are.

- **Work the Keys into the curriculum:** Your students will remember the Keys better if they are brought up repeatedly in various contexts and constantly woven into the curriculum. Once you begin using the Keys, you'll find it easy and natural to work them into your lesson plans.

  - It is fairly easy to integrate the Keys into the **humanities and current events.** With any piece of literature you can ask *What Key is the main character using? What Key is he violating? What Key is represented in the moral or theme?*

  - In **history** lessons, do the same. Ask how historical figures upheld the Keys. *Were they committed to their cause? Did they use Flexibility to achieve their goals? Was there a Key they ignored that would have been beneficial, perhaps even changing their outcomes?*

  - **Writing** assignments and journals are easily tied to the Keys. Simply ask your students to write about the Key you are focusing on, including a definition of the Key, what it means to them and an example of how they use it in their own lives. Many of the stories you'll find in this book are student responses to these simple questions.

– **Science, math, and music** also offer opportunities to reinforce the Keys. Examine the lives of scientists, mathematicians, and musicians and the Keys they used to make their breakthrough discoveries or develop unique musical styles.

• **Find creative ways to focus on the Keys:** Carole Allen, the educator mentioned previously who has been using the 8 Keys in her classrooms for many years, has given us some additional ideas for using the Keys in the classroom.

– Select one Key for students to focus on for the day. Before the end of the day, have students do a "paired share" with another student, chatting about how they lived that Key during the day and/or a time when they forgot to live the Key.

– Keep a permanent chart on the wall with students' names listed down the side of the chart and the Keys going across the top. As the day goes on and students do something that illustrates one of the Keys, for example, Speaking with Good Purpose, then the teacher or the student can go to the chart and put a plus sign showing that the Key was present in the classroom that day.

– Have your students be observers and data collectors by watching older or younger students at play and charting Key behaviors with a plus or minus sign. Turn this into an averaging lesson.

– Have your students score you daily or weekly on your use of the Keys. It empowers them and gives you great feedback.

– Have students browse through newspaper articles and use colored markers to write the Key or Keys that are significant along with a plus or minus sign to indicate a positive or negative application of the Key.

– Have students make a list of their favorite characters (movie, cartoon, sitcom or whatever works for their age group) and discuss what Keys stand out for that character and which ones they need to work on.

– Have a Key celebration at the end of the year where all your students earn a ribbon with the Key they most positively and consistently represent. What a great way to celebrate in front of parents!

Another way to bring the 8 Keys into your classroom is through *Communities of Excellence – Living the 8 Keys,* an initiative of Learning Forum International that unites community leaders, businesses, organizations, educators and parents in character-building school programs. For additional information please refer to the last page of this book or www.CommunitiesOfExcellence.org.

The 8 Keys of Excellence in Your Organization

The 8 Keys of Excellence can be used in nearly any group or organization, including large and small businesses, schools and school districts, departments, teams, clubs, etc. In numerous organizations, the Keys have helped to produce a positive shift in the culture and alignment of the group. To give you a few ideas for your group, here are some of the steps we use at Quantum Learning Network to introduce the 8 Keys to employees and make them an integral part of the company's culture and the lives of the employees.

- **Introduce the 8 Keys at staff meetings and/or management training:** Explain the 8 Keys and the positive effect they can have on your organization's culture. Gain alignment and commitment to using and living the Keys.

- **Display the 8 Keys:** Put key posters where staff and visitors will see them, including reception area, lunchroom, conference room, or other common areas.

- **Discuss the Keys with potential employees:** During the interview process discuss the Keys with potential employees and point out their relevance in your organization.

- **Take periodic assessments:** At Quantum Learning Network, we occasionally do an assessment to determine how well we are living the Keys as an organization. All staff members are asked to complete the assessment form (copy on next page). When the results are compiled we discuss areas that are working well and areas that need improvement. If we all feel we're living the 8 Keys, it's time to celebrate!

- **Give reading assignments on the 8 Keys:** You can assign staff members to read a chapter a week from this book as a way to acquaint them with the Keys. Other suggested

8 Keys of Excellence
Assessment

	Always	Mostly	Sometimes	Almost never

Integrity
I have positive personal values.
My words and actions reflect my values.
I do the right thing.

Failure Leads to Success
I believe that failures are opportunities for growth.
I take time to learn from mistakes and do better
   next time.
I am not fearful of making mistakes.

Speak with Good Purpose
I am aware of the power of my words.
I think before I speak and choose my words carefully.
I speak honestly and kindly.

This Is It!
I focus my attention on what I'm doing right now.
I look for advantages and possibilities in all situations.
I make the most of every moment.

Commitment
I have a clear vision and believe in my ability to
   achieve it.
I take positive action to move forward toward my
   goals.
I persevere—giving up is not an option.

Ownership
I take responsibility for my words and actions.
I "own" the choices I make and the results that follow.
I make positive choices.

Flexibility
I keep my goals in view and watch for what's
   working and what's not working.
When something isn't working I try a different
   approach.
I am willing to adapt to changing situations in order
   to move forward.

Balance
I stay aware of what's meaningful and important in
   my life.
I make positive choices about how I spend my time.
I balance my activities to nurture my mind, body,
   and emotions.

reading could include *Quantum Success: 8 Key Catalysts to Shift Your Energy into Dynamic Focus* by Bobbi DePorter.

• **Reinforce the Keys regularly:** Bring up the Keys at weekly office meetings. Begin each meeting by allowing members to share stories about how they have been living the Keys. Or choose a Key to focus on each week. Assign a staff member the task of giving a short presentation on that Key, including a definition, a story that illustrates it, or an activity that teaches it. At the next meeting, bring the Key up again, asking staff members to talk about how they used the Key during the week and whether they feel it is being used throughout the organization. The point is to increase awareness.

The stories included in this book are written by educators, students, parents, business people, and SuperCamp staff. They describe real-life experiences of living the 8 Keys of Excellence. We hope you find them entertaining, enlightening, and inspiring.

Enjoy!

1

Integrity

Integrity

Match behavior with values

Demonstrate your positive personal values in
all you do and say. Be sincere and real.

Living in integrity is about always making sure that your words and actions align with your values. Values are the things that you believe in – concepts like honesty, commitment, and compassion. If you value honesty, you tell the truth; if you value commitment, you do "whatever it takes" to reach your goal; if you value compassion, you are caring toward others. That's Integrity.

There's a concept in geometry that explains the Key of Integrity very well – congruence. When two shapes are identical in size and shape, they are congruent. One shape fits exactly over the other. When your behavior and values are congruent, you have Integrity. In other words, your behavior matches your values.

Why live in integrity? Who will know if you tell a "little white lie?" Who cares if the cashier undercharges you – it's your gain and her loss, right? It may seem like a small incident, but disregarding your values has repercussions: a nagging conscience, a loss of trust or a disappointed look from a friend who knows you're not telling the truth. These events are remembered, and can eventually affect your reputation and self-esteem.

Living in Integrity means having a clear conscience and a strong character, and feeling good about yourself. Your actions are an expression of what you believe in. People see through your actions that·you are honest, committed, and compassionate. Consequently, they come to trust you; your relationships are solid. As your reputation and self-esteem rise, so does your success.

The concept of integrity sounds simple, but there is one catch. Before you can follow your values, you need to ask yourself, "What do I value?"

Take some time to reflect on this question. Do your current actions support your values or are they in conflict with your beliefs? What do your current actions say about you? Do you show up as honest and committed, or dishonest and wishy-washy? Are you spending your time with the people or activities you value, or is your focus elsewhere? You may say your family comes first, but spend your time on work and social engagements. You may claim to value academics and learning, but are more likely to be partying than studying. What steps do you need to take to align your actions with your values?

Clarifying your values and committing to them will help you reach your goals. People who are successful have a clear set of values to steer them in the right direction. Their values are aligned with their goals, and consequently they are more successful.

Integrity is an expression of who you are.

If you value...

Honesty – be truthful

**Keeping
your word** – follow through

Being fair – do what you expect
others to do

Living in integrity is not always easy, but the benefits are great. It gives you power, self-respect, and the respect and trust of others. When your values and behavior are aligned, you are more likely to find success in life. Stay in integrity, and your values will support you in reaching your goals.

Staff Model Integrity
Bobbi DePorter

When we teach the 8 Keys at SuperCamp, our staff is expected to exemplify these values. They model the behavior they want to see in the students. In the beginning, it's just part of the job for many of them, but over the course of the summer they begin to internalize the Keys and the values start to carry over into all aspects of their lives.

The following letter is an example of the type I receive from staff members who felt out of integrity when they broke a Key. Even though they no longer worked at SuperCamp, the realization of the importance of the Keys made such an impact that they were inspired to write us about it.

Dear Bobbi DePorter,

I wanted to let you know what a difference the 8 Keys have made in my life. Last summer, I worked at the Stanford site as a team leader. I feel I did a good job with my campers and upheld the 8 Keys while at camp. However, to me it was just part of the job and when camp was over I didn't think much about it any more.

I returned to college and my old group of friends were expecting things to be the same as last semester. They were the same, but I wasn't.

Let me explain what I mean. I was hanging out with some friends in the dorm one day and we started talking about a girl down the hall that we always enjoy cutting down when she isn't around. We talk about her boyfriends – "Did you see that creep?" – and her clothes – "If that skirt were any shorter, she'd get arrested" – you get the picture. I used to enjoy it, but this time it made me uncomfortable. Even though I wasn't at camp, Speak with Good Purpose kept popping into my mind.

This is just one incident. When I stay out too late and skip class the next day, or have a bad attitude, or gossip, the Keys keep coming to mind. Now that I am aware of the Keys and have had to teach and practice them at camp, I feel compelled to uphold them throughout my life. I guess that's Integrity.

Well, I just wanted to let you know what an impact your program has made on me. Thank you! I'll be back next summer!

Sincerely,
Carrie L., Stanford Team Leader

Staff members like Carrie discovered that integrity is more than good actions alone. It is a heartfelt belief in these values and a true desire to uphold them.

A Lesson in Honesty
Rickey Maxwell

Several years ago my wife and I, with our three young daughters, spent a day at the races watching the horses run. We made several wagers throughout the day and won several small bets. On this day there was standing room only. So that we did not get separated in the crowd, my wife and children accompanied me to the window to collect tickets and place wagers on the upcoming race.

On one particular trip to the window the person ahead of me cashed in several winning tickets and left the window, at which time I stepped up to cash in. Upon approaching the counter and beginning my transaction, I noticed he had accidentally left a ticket lying on the counter at the window. I looked around but he was nowhere in sight. Not sure whether it was a winning ticket or not, I handed it in with mine and was surprised to find that it was worth close to $100.00. I excitedly walked away from the counter cash-in-hand and explained this bit of good luck to my children who in turn shared my excitement. But, I also noticed a feeling of guilt and realized that this action was not in line with my value of honesty. I could give my children an example of the "finders, keepers" philosophy, or I could set an example for them and at least make an effort to return the prize to its rightful owner.

Because of the peculiar hat this man had worn and my 6'1" height, he was easy for me to spot once we had taken a few steps in the direction we thought he had walked. He was very grateful and offered a reward, which I refused. I had received my reward, which was the glowing looks of admiration I saw on my daughters' faces, and the opportunity to teach by example the importance of honesty to three impressionable young minds.

Integrity Reveals True Character
Brian Krouse

I have used the 8 Keys this year in many things, but I have used the Integrity Key most of all. I have thrown away all my masks; I let people see me for who I really am and I do not hide behind anything. I no longer lie to myself or to other people. I tell them the truth, but at the same time I make sure that the truth is not hurtful, using the Speak with Good Purpose Key. I have found these two keys easy to match up in my life.

For example, I have a friend who is on the heavy side. She cries a lot about it and she even wanted to kill herself over it. But I found when I really started to get to know her that she is just as beautiful inside as can be. I told her that she is beautiful and I meant it from the bottom of my heart. It really brightened up her life and she is happy again. She may not be all that beautiful on the outside but she is on the inside and I really love her for that. We are best friends now and we support each other through thick and thin.

Honesty
Lindsay LaVelle

Integrity is the primary foundation of all positive acts throughout life. Honesty with one's self, with one's friends, and honesty supporting every action one takes makes an individual admirable, real, reliable, and trustworthy.

I can recall a time when I lied to myself frequently. I told myself things to induce different thoughts, some being falsely positive and others harmfully negative. When I became honest with myself, I learned to love myself – my real self. I found who I was and became much more comfortable with myself.

I have always been honest with other people. I value them so greatly that I have always chosen honesty in order to eliminate the risk of hurting or losing them. Integrity also coincides with commitment in that my word is truly the most powerful tool I have.

When I promise to do something, I have given my word and support it with integrity and commitment. If I break a commitment I break a bond of trust that I earned through integrity.

Since my first experience with SuperCamp, I have grown as a person because I live by my word and create healthy relationships with other people I can trust. The Integrity Key has taught and enforced so much in my life.

Disaster Strikes
Bobbi DePorter

A few years after establishing a business school for entre-
preneurs, my partner and I saw our dream school come to
what we thought was an untimely end. One of our professors
showed us a system that he had developed for making money
in stock options. We monitored it for weeks and were excited to see it actually got the results he promised. We eagerly
began investing money – not just our own, but that of others
as well. So sure were we that the system was foolproof, we
personally guaranteed to investors that they would not lose.
For a while, the system turned in good profits. Eventually,
however, we had so many investors and controlled so many

contracts that we ourselves began affecting the market's trends. The system did not provide for this possibility and one day the market turned against us, causing all our positions to collapse completely. We lost millions of dollars in a matter of days.

Because we had guaranteed to our investors that they would not lose, we had to personally cover the losses. I lost everything. All my money, my house, everything. All I had left in the world was my car, which somehow the lawyers had overlooked. But even by liquidating virtually all of my assets, I could not cover a hundred percent of the losses. So I had to personally call the investors and tell them their money was gone. This was so painful. I remember curling up in the fetal position on the floor between phone calls, trying to muster the courage to make the next call. It was a horrible experience. It seemed to me that everyone was against me, everyone hated me. But, ultimately, I realized that this too had been a learning experience, and in the end, it made me stronger. Some of the worst things I could have possibly imagined actually happened to me, and I survived.

Today, thanks to all my experiences, I understand both sides of business. I know that business involves taking risks as well as reaping rewards. We were naïve players in a field that was out of our area of expertise. We had no business speculating in the market, but we justified it by telling ourselves it was okay since all the money we were making was going to support the good work we were doing.

That whole experience, terrible as it was at the time, actually reinforced for me the principles we taught. I still believed in those concepts and so did the students. In spite of our losses, a new partnership was formed and the school continued.

The stock option crisis spurred me to examine my actions and my values. It showed me where they were incongruent. I value businesses and activities that I believe contribute to people's lives. I valued our schools and programs greatly. It was a compromise for me to be involved in stock options, as the only reason was to gain windfalls of money to support our "other" work. My behavior was not matching my values. We can all learn from each other's mistakes. Ask yourself, "Do my actions match my values?" Learn from mine, and take time now to become aware of your values. This is the first step to greater integrity.

2

Failure Leads to Success

Failure Leads to Success

Learn from mistakes

View failures as feedback that provides you with
the information you need to learn, grow, and succeed.

This Key means changing the way you think about failure.
What message do you send yourself when you fail? Many
people give themselves a thorough berating, telling themselves they're stupid, incompetent, will never succeed, and
therefore must quit trying to reach brave new heights and
stick with what they already know. These people never get
what they really want, but at least they never have to face all
the negative feelings they have connected with failure. But is
it worth it to be this safe?

Without failure, there is no success. Babe Ruth struck out
1,330 times, but he also hit 714 home runs. It took Thomas
Edison over 900 attempts to perfect the light bulb. R.H. Macy
failed seven times before his New York department store
became successful. These are just a few of the "famous failures" who refused to give up. Why? Because they recognized
that failure is only feedback – it is the information we need
to succeed.

By examining each "failure" and using that information to
make adjustments and corrections, you gradually move

toward your goal. Henry Ford said, "Failure is the opportunity to begin again more intelligently." But the moment you accept your failure as final and simply stop trying, that is the moment you truly fail.

The way you see failure influences your chances for success. Society views failure in a negative light; consequently, many people have developed a fear of failure. But fear of failure is a learned response. Young children have no concept of failure. As a toddler, you failed hundreds of times in your attempts to talk, walk, or throw a ball. But instead of giving up, you kept trying, using the information you gained through failures to perfect your skills. It was not until later in life, when someone labeled failure as bad, that it became something to be avoided. Unfortunately, by avoiding failure, you also avoid many opportunities for success.

The only way to overcome a fear of failure is to change your perceptions. Instead of thinking of failure as something horrible, you must learn to think of it as *information.* When you try something and don't succeed, examine what went wrong, change your strategy, and try again. Buckminster Fuller once said, "Humans have learned only through mistakes." In other words, if we're not making mistakes, we're not learning. If we're not learning, we're not growing and we're not reaching our goals. Therefore, mistakes are good! *They are the information we need to succeed.*

·

The only real failure is not learning from your mistakes.

Ask yourself:

What have I learned from
this experience?

::

What value can I find in it?

::

What will I do
differently next time?

Success on the Court
Richard Loeber

Failure Leads to Success was the Key that helped me through a tough situation in my freshman year of high school. That year, I tried out for the basketball team. There were two freshman teams and each team had twelve players. About 75 people tried out for the team. I thought the tryouts went well, but I guess the coaches didn't think so since they cut me. This really bothered me since I felt I did a good job.

By failing, I became even more determined to get on the basketball team for the upcoming year. This became even more of a challenge since my family moved from my home state of

Illinois to Chapel Hill, North Carolina. I did not know the players or the coaches on the new team. I was at a disadvantage because I did not know what the coaches were looking for in a player. At least when I was in Illinois, I had a basic idea of what I needed to work on for the team. I decided to meet this challenge by practicing very hard in all areas, especially since this team had won the State Championship the year before. Every day I worked on different aspects of my game.

When tryouts came, my hard work paid off – I made the team! I had a great time playing and I learned a lot. I am now trying to use the same strategy for my junior year of basketball by continuing to practice daily, learning from my mistakes, and perfecting my skills.

Failure is the Best Teacher
Ryan Day

The best lessons I have ever learned came after failures – or what I perceived to be failures at the time. As a senior in high school I applied to Stonehill College. My grades were not great and my SAT scores (college entrance exams) were awful. However, I thought those things were not very important and I would get in anyway. During my freshman and sophomore years, I remember my parents and brothers telling me to study harder and practice for the SAT. I thought I knew better and didn't listen to what was great advice.

By March of my senior year, my classmates were all receiving their letters from colleges. I was still waiting, thinking "no news is good news." I was wrong. I arrived home from school one day and found a letter from Stonehill College in the mailbox. Excited, I tore open the envelope and read the letter: "We regret to inform you that you will not be admitted to Stonehill College this year."

I was devastated. How could this happen to me? After all, I thought I had worked hard in high school – at least hard enough to get into college. I realized then that I hadn't really worked very hard after all, and I now had to face the consequences of my earlier actions.

As I read and re-read that letter I noticed a possible solution to my dilemma: they suggested I apply again as a transfer student after my first semester in a different college. Wow! What an idea! This letter was not the end. This letter was the beginning. They were giving me the opportunity to improve my scores and try again. It would mean that I would have to work hard and show them that I was able to perform at the college level. I now saw that I had the opportunity to turn my failure into success.

After my first semester at St. Bonaventure University, I applied to Stonehill College and was accepted. Four years later I earned my bachelor of arts degree from Stonehill. As I received my degree, I reflected on how what looked like a failure four years prior had now turned into a great success.

Perseverance Pays Off
Brant Gilbert

It was my first year in high school and the track coach didn't like freshmen. I was always above average in track and this was where I was going to prove it. But that first year the coach never looked at me, and after the year was over I was thinking of quitting.

Come track season the next year I was still a nobody, but I tried again. The coach was surprised by my time during time trials and he stuck me on the junior varsity squad. This was my big chance to show the coach what I could do, so I worked very hard in practice. Eventually I was able to beat the varsity team's times. Then one runner got hurt and I was able to run in his spot. After that I became a regular member of the varsity team and I soon made the anchor spot on the relay team. That year, we made it to the state finals. Our team placed eighth and I got thirteenth in the 200 meter.

I decided I didn't want to be below top ten in the state so the next year I started working hard again. I worked hard at practice, pushing the younger kids who seemed to be in the same place that I was my freshman year. We had one week of rest without a track meet before the district meet. The coach took advantage of it and nearly killed us every practice.

On Thursday, two days before the big track meet, I got sick. I missed practice the next day, and the day of the meet I was so sick I didn't want to move. I thought about not running, but when would I have another chance to show I wanted to run in the state meet? What would become of our district championship if I didn't run? I was capable of scoring over 30 points. I had to run for the team, no matter what my physical state – besides, running is 90% mental. So I got out of bed and went to the meet, feeling so sick I could barely breathe.

But I couldn't give up. I worked as hard as possible for my sickly body. I took seventh in the 100 meter and I thought it was all over, I just couldn't run. But I was letting my team down and I couldn't stand it. The next race was the relay. I ran well, bringing us back from a third-place position to a strong first-place victory. "Maybe I'm not as sick as I thought," I told myself, even though I couldn't breathe after my races. But that didn't matter – I finished first in the 200 meter and helped the team to victory. We ended up taking second in the district overall, but in the state meet we failed to make finals. But I met my personal goal; I made ninth place in the 200 meter. Next year I will practice even harder. Next year I will be first.

A Change in Attitude
Amanda Osman

The 8 Keys are something I think about most of the time. I have used all of the Keys in many aspects of my life and they have all helped and taught me something. But the Key that actually helped me the most is Failure Leads to Success.

After having back surgery two years ago, I was not allowed to play any sports. I have always been active and never missed a sport at my school, seven days a week, healthy or sick. I love to do anything. Though I am not the best at anything I am always willing. I love interacting with people.

My favorite sport is soccer, and has been ever since I was little. My Dad played pro soccer for Egypt and the U.S. I love it, but making the team was always hard for me and still is. It's not because I am bad – but all the coaches say the same thing, "You have an attitude that doesn't contribute to the success of the team." It is the reason why I am not recognized for a lot of things I do. It's something that I could change if I really tried but I always just let it control me.

Last year I made junior varsity soccer team as an alternate – not something everyone wants to be. In my school we travel internationally to play in tournaments, and making alternate and sitting on the bench is no fun at all. But I never let anyone know how I felt; I just took it. We traveled to Jordan and my Mom came along and watched the ten minutes I played during the five days of games. It was really embarrassing.

This year was different. I tried out for soccer, the varsity team. I didn't miss one practice, and I really wanted to make it. I busted myself out there in the 100-degree heat. I made sure I was never negative or did anything wrong to the coach or other players. Then the time for cuts came around and I was cut. I was so hurt, but I didn't show it, I pretended I expected it. I was hurting so badly, like anyone who gets cut from his or her favorite sport. I went and talked to the coach. She told me that her reason for cutting me was exactly what the rest of the world thinks of me – my attitude was bad. I was heartbroken.

Then the time came for the team to leave for a tournament in Kuwait. I was upset because the girl who made the team over me came to only seven practices out of forty-five because she was in the school musical. She was new and didn't even know how to kick a soccer ball, but she made it. I was dying inside.

The day of the trip, I was called out of lunch by our activities director and told that this girl couldn't travel outside the country because she didn't have a visa. He said I was invited to go in her place if I wanted. He had already called my Mom and she said I could go. It was only two hours before the plane was taking off and I couldn't believe it.

While I was making up my mind, all I could think of was how I was so heartbroken last year, and how I felt when I didn't make it this year. It was the most crucial choice I had to make at 17 years old. I was thinking too how I was "invited" to be on the team. It was the worst, but I decided that if I did go I could really show that I wasn't the person the coach thought I was – I could prove her wrong. If I didn't go, she would always have the same impression of me.

So I decided yes, I would go. I was so happy and excited. It was the best trip ever. Our team won first place, and all the girls on the team were so happy that I came because we had a really aggressive defense that ensured not one shot could be scored against us the whole tournament. I was never successful at showing my coach that I was different from what she thought of me, but inside I knew I had changed my ways. Failing to make the team the first time taught me something about myself that I would never have learned if I had not failed – Failure Leads to Success.

What It Means to be a Distinguished Student
Alicia Shamberg

I remember my freshman year clearly. I told myself that the only thing I exist for is to get straight A's and to do nothing but study. I committed myself to my plan and I received all A's and A-pluses that year of high school. Even though I thought I had accomplished a lot, others did not think so. I soon learned that, in fact, I had not accomplished as much as I had thought.

At my school there is an annual award that recognizes excellent grades, service to the community, and service to the school. I thought that with my perfect freshman GPA, there would be no doubt that I would receive the award. Well, the Distinguished Students of 1998 were announced, and much to my dismay, my name was not mentioned. I was shocked. I couldn't believe it. A teacher came up to me later and told me why I didn't receive the award. I didn't have enough community service hours.

I am glad I didn't receive the award that year. Because if I had won, I would feel guilty and wrong. That whole experience taught me a very valuable lesson. The lesson I learned is that failure leads to success. I learned my lesson quickly and as soon as summer began, I became involved in virtually everything I would need to be involved with to become a Valley School Distinguished Student. I set the goal to become one and volunteered in my community and school.

I remember how it felt once it was over and I had finished what I had set out to do almost a year before. I was not surprised, I was not shocked. I knew I could do it and I knew it was all worth it. I learned that grades are not the only things in life or what make us great. I believe that once we know Failure Leads to Success, we are remarkable people. I was very pleased to receive the Valley School 1999 Distinguished Student Award.

Pete Rose's Success
Excerpt from *Quantum Business*

Even those people who are the best at what they do are constantly making mistakes. What sets them apart is their ability to learn from those mistakes so as to avoid making them again.

Baseball player Pete Rose got more hits in his career than any man in over 100 years of major league history. When he didn't swing at a pitch, he made a habit of watching the ball go past him and into the catcher's mitt. Almost nobody does that. Most hitters just watch the ball cross the plate and wait for the umpire's call.

Somebody once asked Rose why he watched the ball until it was caught. His reply: "I want to see what that pitch does – whether it drops or curves, whether it ends up being called a strike or a ball, and why. That way, if it's a strike, the next time I'll know I shouldn't let that pitch go. Next time, I'll swing at it."

Rose also liked to go to the plate with a clean, black bat. Why? Because when he hit the ball, it would leave a visible mark, and later he could examine the mark and know how much he was off his swing. He could make an adjustment, and next time hit the ball more solidly. Is it any wonder he got over 4,000 hits? While other players would strike out, throw the bat down, and curse their mistakes, Pete Rose was constantly learning from his.

New Coke Fiasco
Excerpt from *Quantum Business*

Most highly successful business people got where they are after making a few mistakes – even when the mistakes were whoppers. Remember the infamous "New Coke" fiasco when the company launched a new product in an effort to combat Pepsi's growing popularity and reverse Coca-Cola's 20-year market-share decline? The man responsible for this historic blunder was Sergio Zyman, Coca-Cola's marketing "genius." Despite the extensive market research he conducted, the thousands of taste tests, the careful test marketing – when New Coke came out, fans of the old Coke were incensed. They didn't care for the new product at all. After faltering sales, the product was removed from the shelves and replaced by "Coke Classic," which is nothing more than old Coke relabeled.

Embarrassed by the fiasco, Zyman left Coca-Cola in disgrace a year after the incident. But he began his own consulting business and developed it into a profitable venture. A few years later, surprisingly, Coca-Cola wooed him back. Why on earth would a company want to rehire someone who made the biggest mistake in a hundred years of its history? Management felt it was the company's reluctance to tolerate mistakes that had made it non-competitive. They had come to understand that if the main motivator behind something is the avoidance of failure, the result will be inactivity.

In the end, the company found success in the New Coke failure. When old Coke returned to the market, the company experienced its biggest-ever surge in sales, not only reversing the market-share decline, but propelling it to even greater dominance. With that kind of result, some executives have joked, the company should make mistakes like that more often.

Colonel Sanders' Story
Excerpt from *Quantum Business*

Harlen Sanders, founder of the Kentucky Fried Chicken restaurant chain, faced many failures before he reached success, but he never gave up on his dream. In fact, the idea to sell his chicken recipe was born out of failure. When the transportation department rerouted the main highway through his town, the small restaurant he owned went out of business. Bankrupt at the age of 65, "Colonel" Sanders sat on his front porch and opened his first Social Security check – a measly $95. Not knowing how he would survive, he prayed for an answer. "God, if you want me to live like this, I will. But if you've got something else for me to do, let me know what it is." Then he got the idea to share his chicken recipe with others.

He started out by traveling across country in an old clunker of a car, trying to sell his recipe to other restaurants. He knocked on 1,009 doors, and heard the word "no" 1,009 times, before someone finally said "yes."

His first franchise agreements required restaurant owners to pay him five cents for every chicken they sold. After many changes and innovations, Kentucky Fried Chicken restaurants were up and running across the country. Thanks to his perseverance and an ability to find value in the failure of his first roadside restaurant, the Colonel became one of the richest men in the restaurant business. In 1964 he sold Kentucky Fried Chicken to a group of investors for $2 million and an annual salary of $40,000. The salary later rose to $200,000 per year. Not bad for a man who, nine years earlier, was facing the prospect of living out his final years on 95 bucks a month.

3

Speak with Good Purpose

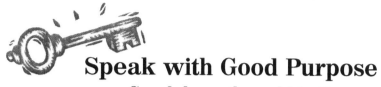

Speak with Good Purpose

Speak honestly and kindly

Think before you speak. Make sure your
intention is positive and your words are sincere.

Words are powerful! Each day we are bombarded with hundreds of thousands of them. Words have the power to build up and break down. They can uplift and enlighten or depress and destroy. We all have control over the words we use and must learn to choose them carefully.

Speaking with Good Purpose is the skill of speaking in the positive and using honest and direct communication. It means focusing on positive conversation and empowering words and avoiding negatives like gossip, complaints and profanity. When a conflict arises, resolving it in a mature manner that maintains good relationships is also a part of this Key.

Speak with Good Purpose is a phrase that comes from a Native American philosophy of positive communication. In the first selection in this chapter, Rolling Thunder describes his peoples' attitude toward positive and negative speech. He states that we are responsible for our thoughts and words, and though it takes effort, we can control both.

Rolling Thunder tells us that if we think certain thoughts, we don't have to say them. Just as we don't take every desirable thing we see, we don't say each thought that enters our minds. We must begin by "watching" our words and "speaking with good purpose only." There is a choice and we must consciously make it.

The first step is awareness. Become aware of the negative thoughts that come to mind. Although there is little use in condemning yourself for these thoughts and ideas, you can learn to control them. When you find that unwanted thoughts have invaded your mind, just realize that you can think what you choose and pay no attention to the irritating interrupters. If they return, just let them alone and say, "I choose not to have these thoughts" and soon they'll go away.

In order to say only what we wish to, we must think before we speak. Once again, self-awareness is crucial and constant practice is necessary. Focus on communicating positive experiences, point out people's strengths, and offer praise and encouragement to others. Of course, there are times when negative feelings and experiences need to be discussed, and these times must be handled carefully. Honest and direct feedback can be powerful and build trust. Think about the intention behind your words. Are they meant to support the person and build a stronger relationship? Focus on the solution, not the problem. Speaking with Good Purpose is extremely important if we want to maintain good relationships. After all, relationships revolve around what is and isn't said!

To truly experience the power of this Key, introduce it to your family, workplace, or school. This Key fosters a positive

Speaking with Good Purpose is the cornerstone of healthy relationships.

Communicate with:

Positive intent

::

Honesty

::

Directness

emotional environment where people are happier, more productive, and more likely to succeed. Often, negative communication is so ingrained that it becomes *the way* to interact with others. We don't give it a second thought. Employees gather in the lunchroom and automatically begin complaining about their day. Students swear or spread gossip to impress their friends. This type of communication not only brings people down, it creates an unproductive environment that fosters negative thinking and stifles learning. Do your best to ban this type of communication from your environment and encourage others to use the Key of Speak with Good Purpose.

Words are tools we use to influence as well as communicate. We can use them to build others up and improve our own outlook. We can speak to bring clarity and beauty, hope and peace to the world, rather than embarrassment, pain or fear. The act of being conscious of our words is the first step. With determination and awareness we can learn to use our words to support, clarify, and strengthen. We can Speak with Good Purpose and reap the many benefits of using this excellent Key.

Speaking With Good Purpose Only
Excerpt from *Rolling Thunder*

People have to be responsible for their thoughts, so they have to learn to control them. It may not be easy, but it can be done. First of all, if we don't want to think certain things we don't say them. We don't have to eat everything we see, and we don't have to say everything we think. So we begin by watching our words and *speaking with good purpose only*. There are times when we must have clear and pure minds with no unwanted thoughts and we have to train and prepare steadily for those times until we are ready. We don't have to say or think what we don't wish to. We have a choice in those things, and we have to realize that and practice using that choice. There is no use condemning yourself for the thoughts and ideas and dreams that come into your mind; so there's no use arguing with yourself or fighting your thoughts. Just realize that you can think what you choose. You don't have to pay any attention to those unwanted thoughts. If they keep coming into your head, just leave them alone and say, "I don't choose to have such thoughts," and they will soon go away. If you keep a steady determination and stick with that purpose you will know how to use that choice and control your consciousness so unwanted thoughts don't come to you anymore.

A Few Kind Words
Megan Kaufman

When I was a senior in high school, there were two cheer-leaders who went to a party over the summer. One was a junior and one was a senior. This may not sound that unusual – after all, people go to parties all the time. Well, this party got out of hand. It was written up in the newspaper and was on the TV news. These two cheerleaders had gotten themselves into a bad situation. There were all sorts of rumors about what went on at the party. One of the most popular stories involved the girls eating dog food.

Well, when school started in September, you can imagine how the gossip mill started churning. These two girls, who were supposed to be popular cheerleaders, were suddenly ostracized by the entire school. People talked about them behind their backs, made jokes to their faces, laughed at them, pointed and whispered, or simply ignored them. Whenever they went to cheer at football games, students from other schools barked and threw dog food at the girls. Finally, after a month, one of the girls could not take it anymore. Karen transferred to a school outside the district. The other girl was a senior. Sara did not want to leave and try to start all over at a new school. These were people she'd gone to school with for years. Surely they would forgive her and forget about all this mess.

The year went on and people did not forget. People did not forgive. While the gossip and teasing lessened, Sara was never allowed to forget that she made a terrible mistake. Of course, to some of her classmates, the mistake was getting caught. They partied, but they never were written up in the paper.

I was not friends with either of these girls. I was not that concerned with Karen's transfer. Sara was in a couple of my classes throughout high school – a biology class, a physical education class, a math class, and things like that. We had not gone to grade school or junior high together. I didn't know her well, but she had always seemed nice enough. I had always said "Hi" to her in the hallway and maybe chatted briefly in the bathroom. I saw everyone treat her terribly after this party. Now, I would love to be able to say that I felt her pain and was angered by the injustice with which she was treated and went out of my way to befriend her and turn the school's opinion of her around. I was, however, a high school senior. I did realize the way people treated her was unfair. I did feel bad for her. But, I had other things to worry about. I did not go out of my way to befriend her, but I did not change my behavior either. I continued to say hi. I continued to chat briefly, but I did not see her much since I didn't have any classes with her.

When graduation night came around, I was practicing my valedictorian speech and adjusting my cap when I felt a tap on my shoulder. I turned around and found myself face to face with Sara. I smiled and said, "Hi! I must look like an idiot talking to myself, huh?" I laughed. She smiled, looked at the ground, and looked back at me. Finally, she spoke.

"I just wanted to say thank you."
"Huh?"
"I wanted to say thank you and I figured I wouldn't be able to find you after we graduated."
"You want to thank me? For what?" I asked.
"I wanted to thank you for being my friend."

I was completely bewildered. I thought she must have mistaken me for someone else. I wasn't her friend. I hardly ever spoke to her. Before I could speak, Sara continued.

"You know, after that party last summer, everyone left me. No one talked to me anymore. All my friends that I'd gone to school with since grade school treated me like I was dirt, or worse. People pointed and laughed. It never got much better as the year went on. You were the only one who stayed my friend. You still talked to me. You still treated me like I was a person. Someone who mattered. It's been almost a year since that party. I still have Terri, John, my boyfriend, and you for my friends. Thank you."

At a loss for words, I nodded and finally whispered, "You're welcome." Sara smiled and said, "Good luck on your speech tonight! See ya!"

And with that, she was gone. I stood there and watched her as she blended in with the rest of my classmates in black graduation gowns. The rest of my *friends* in black graduation gowns. Not to brag, but I had more friends than I could count. I'd always been fortunate that way. Suddenly, none of that mattered. I was still stunned that this girl I felt I hardly knew, a girl I would not have called my friend three minutes ago, considered me a close and valued friend. Could words really hold so much power? Obviously they could. Obviously they did.

I gave my speech. I graduated. I did not see Sara after the ceremonies. I never saw Sara again. I saw her wedding photo in the newspaper a couple of years later; she had married her high school boyfriend. While she thanked me for my friendship that night in June, I often silently thank her for showing me how important words can be. Sara unknowingly taught me a valuable lesson. It has been a lesson I constantly think of as time goes by. So thank you, Sara.

Friendship
Ian Jackson

My best friend is the best listener I've ever known. I can tell her anything that's on my mind and she listens without judging. She helps me make my way through any problems I have, instead of telling me what I should do. She's somebody I have fun with, no matter what we do. She's somebody I learn from and learn with all the time. She inspires me.

What makes her my best friend though, is that she challenges me. She lets me know how I'm showing up to the world, and asks me if that's how I want to be showing up. She tells me what I need to hear, not what I want to hear. She'll tell me when she is proud of me, and she'll also tell me when she thinks I'm making a bad decision. She's never 'nice' – NICE, as she reminds me, stands for Nothing Inside Cares Enough. She's not afraid to tell me that a shirt doesn't look as good on me as another shirt, and she's also not afraid to tell me that I've done a great job on something and that she's impressed. That's so important to me because we are both in a position where we can be completely honest with each other. We've made a choice not to finish a conversation until any negative feelings that have come up are resolved. We are very clear in our communication with each other, and to me that's the most important part of any friendship.

The reason it works so well is because we both know how it's intended. We're friends, not buddies, and we want each other to succeed, not to fail. So when she tells me I could be doing something in a better way than I am, I thank her. When she tells me I need to take a shower, I thank her. When she tells me I need to blow my nose, I thank her.

And by willing me to succeed, and by showing her support for me, she gives me so much strength. She uses words with real purpose, to uplift and enlighten, not to hurt or put down. Her words build trust rather than harm it. That's what real friendship is about.

Sarcasm
Shari Lyman

Speak with Good Purpose has made a huge difference in my life. When I went away to college I became extremely sarcastic. Whoever I met got a taste of my sarcasm. I was always concerned about what other people thought of me, so I covered up this insecurity by joking around with people.

When I returned home for the summer I hung around my best friend from childhood, Danielle. We would go out for lunch, see movies, or shop at the mall. Unfortunately, another bad habit I picked up at college was looking like a slob. When my best friend and I went out, she showered and put on makeup – she looked great! I, on the other hand, looked like a slob. Every time we went out I made a sarcastic comment about how dressed-up she was. I thought if I made a joke about it, I would feel better about how sloppy I looked. This continued throughout the summer.

Over Christmas break Danielle called me and informed me that my comments over the summer really hurt her feelings and if they didn't stop, she couldn't be a part of this friendship any more. I was shocked. I had no idea that my little "jokes" were actually hurting her. I never meant to hurt Danielle.

From that moment on I realized that the words that come out of my mouth have a great impact on the people that I come into contact with. Today, Danielle and I still have a very close friendship. I am thankful I learned that sarcasm can hurt people before I became a teacher and stepped into a classroom full of 27 young children. Following the Key of Speak with Good Purpose has made a difference in the relationships I have with adults and with my students.

His Words Hurt for a Lifetime
Jane Clifford

The San Diego Union-Tribune, March 25, 2000
(Reprinted with permission)

It was one of those casual conversations that just happen.
There were three or four of us, acquaintances who run into
each other at the office several times a week.

We all had a few minutes to shoot the breeze and the subject
turned to clothes. Dresses, to be precise. I don't wear them
very often, they observed. Right, I said, and before I knew it,
I was telling them about a long-ago summer day in Florida. I
was 8 years old, fighting the high humidity in as few clothes

as possible. My grandfather turned to me and said, "Jane, your legs look like strings with flat irons tied to the bottom of them."

The other women laughed. So did I. But we all agreed it really wasn't funny.

"That's awful," one said.

You know, it really was, though my grandfather never meant it to be. My mother gently reprimanded her father and just as gently tried to counter his words with supportive ones of her own.

He was teasing, she said, being playful. I knew that, but I also knew that the little mantra I sang as a child – "Sticks and stones will break my bones but names will never hurt me" – wasn't going to help.

I can see my "bird legs" in old family photos and the truth really does hurt.

Still does.

To this day, every time I put on a skirt or shorts or a bathing suit, I can still hear my grandfather's words.

I suppose being so self-conscious umpteen years later is my problem, but that childhood experience helped me learn the power of words.

My colleagues and I talked about that, too, on our short break. They all have their own memories of things said innocently to them. Truth is, we all probably do. Stuff happens.

But we all agreed on something else that day. That whenever possible, we have to think before we open our mouths to children. And it's not easy.

I know.

My second daughter had an uncanny ability to find a full glass of milk on the table, even if it was at someone else's place, and manage to knock it over. Subscribing to the don't-yell-over-spilled-milk philosophy, I simply had her clean it up and we moved on. But I do remember saying things such as, "Good Lord, Shannon, you knock something over every day."

The result? Uh-huh, she started knocking something over every day, a whole pitcher of Kool-Aid one day. Started calling herself a klutz. I didn't argue with her. Mistake number two.

It took me a while to realize my role in her awkwardness and when I stopped commenting on her spills and started noticing the times she didn't spill…well, you know what happened.

You'd think I'd have remembered that when daughter number three came along and wrote the book on forgetfulness. Glasses at home, sweat shirts at school, books due at the library, homework due to the teacher. You name it, she forgot it. And I forgot what I had learned with her big sister.

"You'd forget your head if it weren't attached," I said to her with a chuckle. I could see Lauren wasn't chuckling with me.

Like her sister, she went on to show me the power of my words to become a self-fulfilling prophecy.

But then one day she got tired of it.

"Mom, it doesn't help if you say that," said the feisty then 10-year-old. "It makes me forget more."

I'm sure it did. So we talked, about how I could help her, about how I may have hurt her. I told her that I knew how she felt, how her great-grandfather had made me feel when I was about her age.

"See!" she said, cutting me no slack, as usual.

My colleagues laughed at that and so did I. We reminisced a little longer, remembered the words that had made us feel good and bad, marveled at their influence so many years later.

I'm thinking maybe I ought to try wearing a dress once in a while.

Improving Family Life with Positive Communication
Anna Fox

I use the 8 Keys every day in my life. The one that I utilize most is also the one that was hardest for me to do before I went to SuperCamp. That Key is Speaking with Good Purpose. I now use this Key in my home life as well as my school life.

I have a younger brother who I used to argue with constantly. I have also had difficulty controlling my temper, and I disagreed a lot with my mom, dad, and stepfather. After I returned from my awesome experience at SuperCamp, I began to use Speak with Good Purpose to communicate better with my family.

Speak with Good Purpose has also helped me out at school. A particular incident that comes to mind is the time I got in trouble in my Spanish class. My teacher blamed me for being a part of a joke that some of the boys in class had played on her. I hadn't been a part of the joke and so I was a little hurt that she would accuse me of being involved with it. She was furious and wanted to have all of the kids involved suspended. I knew that arguing with her would make it look like I had been involved, and that is not what I wanted. I stayed after class and very calmly told my teacher that I had nothing to do with what had happened. I also apologized because I felt bad about laughing at what the boys had done and said.

After that the teacher always treated me with a higher level of respect. She knew that I respected her and that I was honest and could be trusted. We had a strong relationship and after I passed her class I would often visit just to say hello.

I now realize that if I approach a problem or conflict with love and understanding instead of contempt or anger, the other person will, more likely than not, understand my point of view and want to communicate with me. It is sometimes difficult to swallow my resentment and frustration and address the problem with respect and understanding. However, I have found that choosing the more challenging path through life is always the most rewarding and fulfilling. Since using this Key, my life has changed drastically and I love the change. Speaking with Good Purpose is my favorite Key and I hope to share it with others.

4

This Is It!

This Is It!

Make the most of every moment

Focus your attention on the present moment.
Keep a positive attitude.

Life is full of distractions. You may start out with your day neatly planned, only to find yourself completely off course by the day's end. You may plan on going to the mall and end up babysitting a younger sibling, or look forward to finally completing a pressing project only to find yourself bogged down with phone calls and interruptions. Mired in the unexpected, you grumble, complain, and have a terrible day. You spend your time thinking about what you'd rather be doing, daydreaming, or worrying about some past or future event. Although you're completing the task at hand, your focus is still on the things you *wanted* to do.

Whenever your mind is occupied with something other than what you're doing, you miss what's going on around you in the moment. Opportunities for a valuable experience are lost. As you're waiting for the next moment to arrive, the present slips away.

But there is a way to turn this type of behavior around. This Is It! means making the most of every moment. It means focusing your attention on the present and giving each task your best effort. It means keeping a positive attitude. This

Key can make a big difference in the way you live your life. It can make each day exciting, productive, and fulfilling.

Sounds like a lot to expect from three little words, but imagine what your life would be like if you made each moment count. What if you spent that babysitting time actually enjoying your little brothers and sisters, playing games, and getting to know them better? Or what if you used those phone calls at work to make new contacts, strengthen relationships, and build your business? Your day would turn from terrible to terrific! You would get more out of school, work, friendships, sports...whatever you're doing at the moment.

Clearly, This Is It! is a powerful tool, but how do you begin putting it to use? The key to making it work in your life is to make it a habit. First, you need to become conscious of when you're not using This Is It! When you catch yourself feeling bored or daydreaming, turn that moment around. It may help to carry something with you as a subtle reminder, or designate a piece of jewelry, such as a watch or ring, to trigger your memory. Whatever it is, when you see it you will make the connection and remember to use This Is It!

Another tool you can use is called reframing. This simply means looking at a negative task or situation from a different angle, or framing it differently. Instead of focusing on the task itself, focus on the outcome, the person you will help or the character you will build by completing the unpleasant project. Find the value in what you're doing and focus on it.

When you start making the present "it" and make the most of every moment, you may rediscover a few things you've been taking for granted. The things you've been dreaming about may be right under your nose. You're certain to make some discoveries and enjoy life more, so why wait for tomorrow? *This Is It!*

Live in the present — make today IT.

By making

something else IT,

you miss what's

going on

around you

in the moment.

Finding Encouragement in a "This Is It!" Attitude
Wesley Canny

Throughout this past year I have utilized the Key, This Is It! I have used it in school and in my extra-curricular activities. It has helped me meet and attack new challenges with success. When I attended boarding school this past year I found that I was unable to rely on my parents' positive encouragement as much as I had in the past. I needed to find positive feelings within myself when I was faced with challenging situations. I was able to make the year a positive and rewarding one by using This Is It!

Initially, I attacked school head-on, but eventually I began to slip back into my old habits. I received a wake-up call when my math teacher questioned my effort. I decided I would challenge myself and put the effort into my homework and schoolwork using the technique I had learned at SuperCamp. I remembered the way I learned best and also the reading techniques, but most of all I decided to make school "It!" It didn't happen right away and at times I did fall back into my old habits, but then I would remember the excitement we all felt at SuperCamp when we met a challenge head-on and conquered it, and I soon found myself back on the right track.

This Key has helped me realize that if I approach challenges, academic or otherwise, with a positive attitude, they don't seem so overwhelming and can usually be worked out in a meaningful way. Each experience and challenge helps prepare me for the next one.

•

Make Your Actions Count
Laurie Boswell

Of all the 8 Keys, This Is It! is the one that stands out for me, and I have applied it in my life for as long as I can remember. To me This Is It! is the chance that may never come again. A moment in time, to pray, to care, to love, to share. Be kind, make a friend, let someone know how you feel. Forgive, say "I'm sorry," make things right. Commend a job well done. Say "Thank you." Remember a face. Share a smile. Give it all you've got, give it your best. Make a difference, one you may never know about. Help a stranger. Make your actions count. Share your life. Have compassion. Love unconditionally. Have no regrets. Count your blessings. No matter how you express it, This Is It!

When I was fourteen years old, my father became ill. He had high blood pressure, which led to the loss of both kidneys. He was put on hemodialysis, a machine that cleans the blood of waste products. Three days a week he was hooked up to the machine for six hours at a time. This went on for four years.

Then a kidney became available that was an exact match for Dad. The transplant allowed him to live another seven years. We worked hard to make sure his quality of life was the best it could be. Through those years, on a day-to-day basis, life and death was often the underlying current. In other words, This Is It! We were blessed to have Dad eleven years longer than maybe we should have.

Dad died in 1983, and no one deserved peace more than he did. He fought long and hard. To this day I have no regrets about my Dad. There wasn't a day we didn't say "I love you," a time we didn't make things right, a moment we didn't make a difference in each other's lives.

Last spring my mother had emergency quadruple bypass surgery. Once again, This Is It was clearly stated in my life. During the many hours of surgery, my sisters and I reflected on our past. There were no regrets. Constantly, we said "I love you, I care, thank you," sharing all parts of our lives. Times like these remind me of just how important This Is It is in my life. Once again, we were blessed and Mom's health was restored. She is well and back at work.

For me, prayer and love, family and friends, all encompass the Key, This Is It!

The Diving Champion
Mike Hernacki

Some people are experts at making their life IT. A marvelous example of this is a young woman from the Midwest whom I greatly admire. In 1983, she was ranked third-best high diver in her state, only 2.5 points behind the first-place diver. Today she's preparing herself to become a world champion high diver. Recently she was given an award for typing 43 words per minute. Most typists know that 43 words per minute is no great accomplishment. But for this woman it is – because she has no arms! Despite a serious handicap, she sees herself as a winner and believes in herself. She sees life as an adventure and makes the most of every moment, stretching her abilities and beliefs about what she can achieve. Rather than letting her handicap limit her, she looks at her situation as a whole and says, This Is It! She then goes on to beat overwhelming odds and accomplish great things.

Economic Slump
Bobbi DePorter

Sometimes This Is It! can help us face a crisis. In 1991, the combination of the Gulf War and the U.S. economic slump caused a sudden decrease in SuperCamp enrollments, hitting us hard financially. We were faced with some difficult decisions about cutbacks and layoffs, but we didn't abandon our basic principle of open communication. We held a meeting with the staff and were honest with them about our financial situation and the impact it would have on them. It was one of the most difficult meetings I've ever had to conduct. I wanted to avoid it, but I had to make it This Is It! and be honest with everyone.

I was amazed by the level of trust and support I received from the staff. Everyone started brainstorming ideas on how we could get through this period. Some people offered to defer their paychecks for three months, and one man even offered to lend us his personal savings. The staff trusted us and strongly believed in the value of our programs. Using This is It, they pulled together to make the most of their resources and keep the company going.

If you can make the most of every moment, you're well on your way to becoming more productive and living a more fulfilling life. Keep in tune with the present moment, and make it count. You only have one life and…This Is It!

•

Making School "It!"
Natalie Vane

My favorite Key by far is This is It! That's the Key I used least often until I went to SuperCamp. Since then, life has been an extremely fun adventure. What will I learn today? C'mon! Gimme that test! I've decided spontaneously to give flowers to my teachers, who have ended up adoring my enthusiasm in their classes. I truly love school now. I keep thinking, This Is It! I'm almost out of high school, and I want to make every moment of my life as fulfilling as possible. Using the This Is It! mentality, I've entered the science fair (and won Honorable Mention), I've entered into a creative "Reflections" contest (another Honorable Mention) and I applied to Latin Governor's School. (Fifty people or less from the entire state get in, and I was one of them!) I'm looking forward to making each day of school "It!"

The Key to Self-Discovery
Lucus Keppel

This Is It! is the Key that I believe applies the most to my life.
Ever since that fateful day at SuperCamp last year when This
Is It! was explained to me, I have struggled to include it in
my life. I have always had the tendency to hide behind a
"mask" so that people would not get to know the real me.
That has changed tremendously. I now know I can be myself,
and if people don't accept me as myself, then there will be
others who will. I find myself trying to explain the concept of
This is It to group members on school projects or to teachers
searching for the right word. Of everything I learned at
SuperCamp, This Is It! has stuck with me the longest. It is

invigorating, knowing that I can be accepted as myself and not be laughed at or ridiculed.

If the entire world used This Is It!, then there would be no need for masks or other forms of communication blocks. Everyone would be themselves, and the world would practically hum with the noise of people finally figuring out their true selves. I know that the world would definitely improve as more and more people started using this Key. Even as I type these words, new people are being born that will need to know about This Is It! and people are dying that never had a chance to learn about it. Eventually, everyone will hear of This Is It!. And the world will see the progress I've been rambling on about.

This Is It! has changed my life so much that I feel as if my old self has gone away and a new, better self has appeared to replace him. No more worries about if a certain clique will accept me, or whether I will have friends today. All I have to think about is keeping a positive mood. And, after I had long thought that optimism was a bad outlook, I found that optimism attracts people – they see an optimist and wonder about the future. Well, I wonder about the future as well, but I know that whatever it brings, I will find opportunities, be optimistic, and give my all to solving the problems I face.

Living Life to the Fullest
Lorian Jenkins

Once in your life you will have some kind of incident that will change you in some way. Whatever the incident might be, it will make you step back from reality for a minute and make you look at how you're choosing to live your life.

On November 3, 1998 at 6:30 a.m., my mom came into my room to find me unconscious and having convulsions. I was taken to Henry Mayo Newhall Hospital, still unconscious, and treated for seizures. After a couple of hours, the pediatrician decided I needed to be airlifted to UCLA for treatment in the Pediatric Intensive Care Unit. I remained in a coma until the following morning, when I slowly began to wake up.

After I had undergone many tests, the neurologist determined that I had allergic "idiosyncratic central nervous system reaction" to a prescribed medicine that I had taken. The doctors transferred me back to Henry Mayo Newhall Hospital to finish my recovery.

In those short, upsetting five days I learned life lessons that I will carry with me through the rest of my life. Through all the support my parents gave, to all the visitors, get-well cards, flowers, and phone calls, I learned how truly precious life is.

It has been seven months since I was hospitalized, and in those months I feel I have lived every moment of my life to its fullest. Some people may think life is just a headache, but I now look at it as a challenge. You may not always overcome those challenges, but it is the hard work and determination that you put into it that is important. You will never know if you are going to have another chance to overcome that obstacle.

Most people will go through a change, but sometimes tend to fall back on their old approach to life. I still occasionally feel frustrated and discouraged in my daily life, but then I look back and remember how I almost didn't have the opportunity to experience those feelings again. The lesson I learned from this situation is not to frown in discouragement at your problems, but smile with a rowdy grin. In other words, This Is It!, so live your life to the fullest.

Ancient Finnish Sauna Provides Life Lesson
Duane Grischow

In the fall of 1989 I began my one-year global tour with Up With People. When I was just about to leave my house my mom gave me one piece of final advice. She said, "Duane, during your year of international travel you'll have many opportunities to explore and experience many new things. Some of those things may be very different from our American culture. However, the key is to at least try everything."

Since I was a staff member with SuperCamp for several years I knew exactly what she meant. At SuperCamp it's called This Is It! (making the most of any moment).

My tour challenged me with This Is It! many times. However, my moment of truth happened that January when I arrived in Finland.

Quickly my host mom and dad, Pirjo and Timo, introduced me to Finnish sauna. As an American I associated sauna with health clubs. However, I quickly learned sauna had a different twist and a greater historical meaning for Finnish people.

Timo said, "Finns love sauna! One out of three Finns has a wood-burning sauna in their house. Sauna is very important to Finnish history. It was the sauna that provided the moral strength for the Finnish to defeat the powerful Russian army and gain independence in our country."

Although I did gain a greater appreciation for the historical value of Finnish sauna, what I truly experienced was a life-time lesson I still use to this day. Timo said, "Duane, this is how Finns experience sauna. We grab our favorite beverage and go in the sauna for a few minutes. Then we go and roll in the snow and run quickly back into the sauna and warm up. We do this process several times over an hour. We feel the experience cleanses the mind and soul."

My first response was, "Roll in the snow!" The little voice in my head was really turning up the volume. Remember January in Finland consists of dark nights, lots of snow, and sub-zero temperatures. Rolling in the snow with my bare skin was not my first choice.

However, right away I shut out the little voice. I remembered my mom's advice, "Try everything." I also remembered what

I had learned about taking advantage of the moment and making the opportunity This Is It!

I decided to roll in the snow. It was a little tingly at first. However, I felt so alive. I was hooked. I was like a true Finn. From that point forward, I looked forward to enjoying sauna with all my Finnish host families.

The moral of the story is that so many times in life we're looking for "flashier moments." We're always looking for something better or more comfortable around the corner. As a result we miss out on so many incredible moments right in front of our eyes. Some of those moments are with the ones we love the most (our spouse, siblings or parents).

I almost missed out on one of the most unique experiences in Finnish heritage because of a closed mind. However, a simple mind-shift and creating This Is It! in the moment cemented a lifetime learning memory. Ten years later I still use Finnish sauna as a metaphor for creating opportunities of This Is It in my everyday life.

The Value of Time
Unknown

Imagine there is a bank that credits your account each morning with $86,400. It carries over no balance from day to day. Every evening deletes whatever part of the balance you failed to use during the day. What would you do? Draw out every cent, of course!

Each of us has such a bank. Its name is TIME. Every morning, it credits you with 86,400 seconds. Every night it writes off, as lost, whatever of this you have failed to invest to good purpose. It carries over no balance. It allows no overdraft.

Each day it opens a new account for you. Each night it burns the remains of the day. If you fail to use the day's deposits, the loss is yours. There is no going back. There is no drawing against tomorrow. You must live in the present on today's deposits. Invest it so as to get from it the utmost in health, happiness, and success.

The clock is running. Make the most of today.

To realize the value of ONE YEAR, ask a student who failed a grade.

To realize the value of ONE MONTH, ask a mother who gave birth to a premature baby.

To realize the value of ONE WEEK, ask the editor of a weekly newspaper.

To realize the value of ONE HOUR, ask the lovers who are waiting to meet.

To realize the value of ONE MINUTE, ask a person who missed the bus.

To realize the value of ONE SECOND, ask a person who just avoided an accident.

To realize the value of ONE MILLISECOND, ask the person who won a silver medal in the Olympics.

Treasure every moment that you have. And treasure it more because you shared it with someone special, special enough to spend your time on them. And remember that time waits for no one.

Yesterday is history. Tomorrow is mystery. Today is a gift. That's why it's called the present.

If I Had My Life to Live Over
Nadine Stair, age 85

I'd dare to make more mistakes next time.
I'd relax.
I would be sillier than I have been this trip.
I would take fewer things seriously.
I would take more chances.
I would climb more mountains and swim more rivers.
I would eat more ice cream and less beans.
I would perhaps have more actual troubles, but I'd have
   fewer imaginary ones.
You see, I'm one of those people who live sensibly and
   sanely hour after hour, day after day.
Oh, I've had my moments, and if I had it to do over again,
   I'd have more of them. In fact, I'd try to have nothing else.
Just moments, one after another, instead of living so many
   years ahead of each day.
If I had it to do again, I would travel lighter than I have.
If I had my life to live over, I would start barefoot earlier in
   the spring and stay that way later in the fall.
I would go to more dances.
I would ride more merry-go-rounds.
I would pick more daisies.

Commitment

Commitment

Make your dreams happen

Take positive action.
Follow your vision without wavering.

Commitment is the breathtaking moment of making a compelling decision, jumping in, and going forward with gusto. It's the magic moment when all hesitation is left behind. You begin a climb that leads to amazing new heights, beyond what you have imagined.

History is full of examples of the power of commitment. William Hutchinson Murray, of the Scottish Himalayan Expedition of 1950, wrote:

Until one is committed, there is hesitancy, the chance to draw back, always ineffectiveness. Concerning all acts of initiative (and creation), there is one elementary truth, the ignorance of which kills countless ideas and splendid plans: the moment one definitely commits oneself, then Providence moves too. All sorts of things occur to help one that would never otherwise have occurred. A whole stream of events issues from the decision, raising in one's favor all manner of unforeseen incidents and meetings and material assistance, which no man could have dreamt would have come his way. I have learned a deep respect for one of Goethe's couplets:

> *Whatever you can do,*
> *or dream you can, begin it.*
> *Boldness has genius, power,*
> *and magic in it.*

The decisive act of making a commitment sets into motion an energy field that propels you forward on your journey. Obstacles are eventually overcome, and your commitment pushes you on until you reach your goal.

But before you can harness the powerful energy of commitment, you must discover where your commitment lies. Think about what excites you, what spurs you to action. Think about the things you value and the changes you want to make. Discover what your vision is, then commit to making it real. Be willing to throw yourself into it wholeheartedly, to "do whatever it takes."

Anyone who has ever succeeded at something difficult did so by being completely committed to the goal. Strong commitment gives you the power to effect change. Each obstacle you conquer strengthens your commitment and your belief in your vision. Those who have used this Key have literally changed the world.

Commitment is taking positive action to make your dreams happen.

By being

willing to do

"whatever it takes"

you can literally

change the world.

Making the World Work
Excerpt from *Quantum Business*

On a chilly night in the winter of 1927, a young man stood on the shore of Lake Michigan and stared morosely into the icy water. Thinking himself a total failure, he was about to put an end to his miserable life. Twice he had been expelled from Harvard. He had failed at more jobs than most people hold in their lifetimes. And worst of all, he had lost his infant daughter, Alexandra, to spinal meningitis. His pain was so great, he actually took comfort in the prospect of swimming out into the lake and letting himself drown.

But as he stood there thinking the blackest thoughts, he had a profound revelation. In reviewing his life, he realized that although many of his experiences were negative, they were rich in variety and value. He thought about what an incredible storehouse of experiences each person is, and it occurred to him that he might be able to use some of his experiences to help others avoid the hurt that he had known. He decided to see what would happen if he simply began to look at life differently. He wondered what might result if, instead of focusing on himself, he would commit his life to others.

At that moment the young man committed his life to "making the world work." He began to question and examine nearly every aspect of his life, using what he called "experimental evidence" – discovering things for himself using scientific methods, rather than just accepting them as true.

The young man was R. Buckminster "Bucky" Fuller, and his commitment to "making the world work" resulted in some of the greatest achievements of the twentieth century. Out of Bucky's experimentation came many earth-shaking inventions and ideas. The Dymaxion map and the geodesic dome, two of his most famous works, are both based on his concept of Dymaxion: increasing performance using fewer materials – or doing more with less.

During his lifetime, Bucky wrote more than 20 books, held 27 patents, and received 47 honorary doctorate degrees. His work spanned the fields of architecture, design, art, engineering, education, poetry, and mathematics. He has been called the Leonardo da Vinci of our time. All this was due to the commitment he made back in 1927 on that cold, lonely night on the shores of Lake Michigan, to "making the world work."

The GENI Project
Excerpt from *Quantum Business*

Peter Meisen committed himself to turning Buckminster Fuller's idea of a global energy network into reality. Bucky developed a plan wherein each of us would share our energy with others during our non-peak hours at night, thereby insuring there would be enough energy to supply every country with all their needs. Peter started his quest with only himself and very little capital. But a strong commitment is contagious – a magnetic force, pulling others in, gathering momentum and support. That's just what happened with Peter's project.

"The enormity of the project scared me to death," Peter recalls, "because it was too big; obviously beyond any one individual. But I had developed enough confidence in a previous project to approach it – not a lot of experience, but a commitment that this could be done if we just started from what we had.

"The first steps were to educate myself personally to understand the technology. I went to the library and I went to the experts themselves. I went to both Mexico and France to meet with engineers."

In 1986 Peter founded the Global Energy Network Institute (GENI), a nonprofit organization dedicated to realizing Bucky's plan. It took five years to get to GENI's first primary milestone, which was an international workshop in Winnipeg, Manitoba, Canada.

Today the power grid concept has been implemented in countries around the world: across the United States; the Nordal system connecting Scandinavia to the rest of Europe; the British Channel link between France and England; and in the former USSR, across seven time zones (over 10,000 kilometers).

While it's difficult to give full credit to Peter for all of this, the fact is many more countries are now linking power systems, and interconnections are accelerating around the world. Since 1989, many former enemies have laid down their weapons and initiated electrical energy-sharing in rapid succession. It took East and West Germany just two months to interconnect after the fall of the Berlin Wall, and the Washington Declaration between Jordan and Israel added the linkage of power grids as a prime provision in their peace accords.

GENI's mission statement includes the "commitment to improve the quality of life for all without damage to the planet." Millions of people are now aware of this project through the efforts of Peter and the GENI organization, and Peter continues to win supporters from around the world. His story demonstrates the enormous power contained in the commitment of just one person.

The Driving Test
Ian Jackson

At the age of 18, I finally got around to learning to drive. The driving age in Britain is 17, and we don't have "drivers' ed" lessons, so I was paying for classes outside high school. That was the case for everyone, but still most of my friends were already learning. Many had passed their test.

I was not very confident, and after 10 or 12 one-hour lessons, I took my driving test and I failed.

I wasn't surprised. The sheet my test instructor gave me showed that I was very close to passing, and that I did better than I felt I did. Still, I didn't really have any commitment to passing the test. I was taking the test because I felt I should and not because I felt I was ready. I was telling myself throughout the test that I wasn't ready, convincing myself I was right.

I had my final high school exams soon after, but I made a half-hearted effort to try again. Of course, the great Yoda from Star Wars would say, "there is no try. There is only do or do not." Maybe things would have been different if I'd listened to him. My driving test was arranged for the day after my final exam. I didn't practice driving at all during my month-long exam schedule. I told myself I didn't have the time, although I know it was a choice I made.

I failed again. I decided to take a break, and I blamed my instructor. The truth was, I really wasn't committed.

I went away for a year, and then to University in a city where a car would have been more of a problem than a help, and I made a choice to spend my money on other things, more important to me at the time. I always told myself that I would get around to it again sometime.

After the most amazing summer of meeting my best friend and of us both setting goals and supporting each other in reaching them, I decided to pass my test. There was no deciding to try this time. There was only deciding to pass. In ten weeks.

In the first week of our semester, I had my first driving lesson. I hadn't been in the driving seat of a car for over three years, and it felt like I was starting from scratch. The test had been changed into two parts now, so after a few weeks

I applied for my written test on road rules. There was a cancellation for the middle of November, so I went in knowing that I was going to pass. I needed 30 out of 35 to pass. A few days later I got my certificate in the mail. I got 32!

Now I could apply for my practical driving test. I called that day to set up a test, and again there was a cancellation. There were no other tests available for weeks either side, and normally people wait months to get one. I was fortunate, but I had already known that it would work out, because I was committed to making it happen. My driving instructor said that I might not be ready by the time the test came, and I turned and said "I will be."

I took my test on the fifteenth of December – ten weeks to the day after my first lesson. My best friend was with me at the time, giving me a huge amount of support – she was the only person I had told about the test and even the lessons. I loved the idea of surprising people once I had passed.

The test was great. I did fine for the whole 30-minute drive, and I passed with no errors at all!

I reached my goal because I was clear about what it was I wanted. I was so committed to passing that I believed in myself totally. I knew I could do it, and I made it happen. Calling my parents a few minutes later, I gave them a wonderful surprise, and it was such a great feeling.

Now I've got a poster on my wall that I made, saying, "If you believe you can't or if you believe you can, either way you're right." I love that quote and it really helped me so much that day, and every day since.

Doing Whatever It Takes
Ryan Day

Commitment is doing whatever it takes to accomplish a dream or goal. By working my hardest and staying on track I have the ability to become successful.

Being committed is not always an easy thing to do, however, it is a powerful Key that keeps me focused on the aspirations I set for myself.

I was committed to becoming an educator. I knew that in order to teach children I would need a college degree. I was not a good student myself and did not enjoy school, but I knew that attending college was something I had to do to reach my goal. After four years of hard work and commitment, I received my degree.

I graduated from college thinking the most difficult challenge was behind me. I was wrong: I still needed to find a job and put my education to work. The big question was how? Where should I start? I filled out applications, went to interviews and sent out resumes and cover letters, but I was not receiving any offers. I was at a loss.

I took a job at the mall working nights and weekends so that I could support myself while continuing my search for a teaching position. I began to apply at schools as a substitute teacher, thinking that if I could just get my foot in the door I could get a permanent position. Yes, it was tiring working 5:00 p.m. to 11:00 p.m. at the mall, substitute teaching all day at school and spending my weekends back at the mall again. However, it was all necessary. The bills had to be paid and I was committed to my goal. It was a wonderful feeling the day I was asked to interview for a permanent position and an even better feeling to be offered the job and accept it.

Yes, there were times I wanted to give up, but the commitment I had to teaching children and helping them learn to love learning pushed me *through those times. I am very thankful that I had the Key of Commitment to keep me grounded and focused on the goal ahead of me.

Andrew Holleman's Commitment
Excerpt from *Kids with Courage*

Andrew Holleman had practically grown up on the wetlands. He loved its plants, creatures, and gooey mud. One day in 1987, Andy's family received a letter from a land developer. The letter announced the developer's plans to build 180 condominium units near the Hollemans' home in Chelmsford, Massachusetts. Twelve-year-old Andrew snatched the letter and shouted, "He can't do that! He's talking about building right on top of the wetlands!"

Andy knew that several species living on that land were either endangered or on the Special Concern list of animals whose numbers are shrinking. He had spent much of his free time roaming the area, watching great blue herons bend their long, delicate legs in marshy waters, seeing blue-spotted salamanders slither past shy wood turtles, and hearing the red-tailed hawk's lonely call – *cree, cree.* He often ripped off his baseball cap and waved to salute its graceful flight.

"Mom, you've got to take me to the library," Andy insisted. "I need to find out everything I can about the wetlands. We've got to fight this." At the library, Andy examined the master plan for their town. He dug into state laws. He discovered the exact plans for the condo complex, including that the proposed development sat on a stream which led into Russell Mill Pond. The pond fed into town wells. So it was possible that Chelmsford's drinking water could be contaminated, too. He had his ammunition and he had to do something. He thought of all the living things whose habitats would be destroyed by the condos: the ladyslippers, mountain laurels, fringed gentians, foxes, and snakes.

The wetlands were too important to cover with concrete and steel. Andy couldn't allow Pontiacs and Toyotas to replace blue herons and shy wood turtles. He couldn't permit blaring car horns to muffle the *cree* of the red-tailed hawk. "So, I drafted a petition for the residents to sign to try to stop the developer from building," Andy says. "I walked around the neighborhood and collected 180 signatures. I told everyone to come to the public town meeting with the developer."

Andy sent copies of the petition to various officials and wrote letters to senators, representatives, TV reporters, and the Audubon Society, but got no help.

On the night of the town meeting, over 250 people showed up. When the developer stood up and announced that he was the one who had invited everyone, the audience disagreed, saying, "No it was Andy Holleman who invited us here." Andy delivered a speech that the residents responded to with thunderous applause. That was just the beginning of the battle for Andy. The meetings continued for another ten months. There were at least two meetings every week and sometimes more. Andy attended every meeting – and Andy still got high grades in school. He even spoke at most of the meetings. Ten months after he started his campaign to save the wetlands, Andy got the good news that the Board had denied the developer's application to build on the wetlands.

What did all of this mean to Andy? He became a celebrity. Even though he is modest and shy, he accepted invitations to speak at schools, community groups, and organizations. He received many awards, including the Young Giraffe Award for young people who "stick their necks out" for the good of others. His award was a free trip to Russia. Andy is planning to go to college where he'd like to study environmental law. Meanwhile, he's setting up a non-profit fund to purchase the wetlands to preserve them forever. Then he and other people can always wander by Russell Mill Pond, gathering autumn leaves from crimson swamp maples and golden oaks. He can watch the blue herons bend their long, delicate legs in marshy waters, and see blue-spotted salamanders slither safely past shy wood turtles. And he can hear the lonely *cree* of the red-tailed hawk as it soars freely, high above the pond, dipping its wings as if in salute to him.

Excerpt from *Kids with Courage: True Stories About Young People* by Barbara A Lewis © 1992. Used with permission from Free Spirit Publishing Inc., Minneapolis, MN; 1.800.735.7323; www.freespirit.com. All rights reserved.

Swim Team
Alexandra Vaughn

Last year, I was on the school swim team. This was my first time swimming for any reason other than just to have fun. I wanted to become a better swimmer, and I loved being in the water. It would also help me get in shape for track in the spring.

One day, I approached my parents and told them that I wanted to be on the swim team. They were surprised, to say the least, for I wasn't a good swimmer. "If you decide to do this, it will be a huge commitment," they said.

"I know that. I can do it," I replied. They told me to think it over and go to the orientation meeting just to see what it was supposed to be like.

About a week later, there was an orientation meeting at the school for all of the people interested in joining the swim team. I went. The coaches told us the level of commitment they expected from us was one hundred percent. Anyone not willing to make that commitment might as well leave. In my mind, I had already made that commitment. What the coaches said only strengthened my resolve.

They proceeded to tell us how difficult it might be to keep this commitment. They expected good attitudes and a willingness to do as we were told. Also, no staying up late on the night before a meet, no partying, no drinking, no smoking, no drugs. And uphold good morals. There were also high standards for grades. If grades dropped below a certain level, we would go to practice, but sit at a table and do our homework until the grades were brought up. So what? I thought. Easy. This can't be that hard. I don't go to parties or do illegal things anyway, and what's going to bed a few hours earlier once in a while going to hurt?

In the end, I found out how serious this commitment really was. I learned to follow and use the coaches' suggestions. They knew what they were talking about. At one point, about a month into practice, I was not allowed to swim for several weeks because of toe surgery. Everyone told me how hard it was going to be to get back in shape for the meets. They gave me every chance to quit, but I wanted to swim. When I got back in the water, I knew it was my one and only chance to prove to myself and others that I could do it, no matter what.

I gave practice everything I had. I took the coaches' constructive criticism (and believe me, I got a lot of it!) with a smile and tried to do what they instructed.

When the season was almost over, one of the coaches had me swim the 500-meter freestyle in practice. I had come to practice late because of a doctor's appointment. Almost everyone else was done. I swam in a lane next to a girl who regularly swam this distance at meets. I swam the last seven laps by myself, while most of the team watched me. I finished about 30 seconds too late to qualify for district, but my coach was thrilled. She had expected me to take at least five more minutes. The coaches let me have one lane to myself, so I swam another 500-meter freestyle and 150 meter backstroke. I got out of the water 15 minutes after everyone else left, but I just did the extra for fun. That is what commitment did for me. I was proud of what I had done. No one could take that achievement away from me. I had succeeded where everyone else had thought I would fail. I had persevered and swam even when I came in last, and I achieved my goal – to improve and have fun.

Meeting the Big Challenge
Jennifer Myers

While working as a team leader at SuperCamp, I accumulated enough stories and memories to last a lifetime. One incident that I remember very clearly happened with a camper named Susan. Susan's sister had attended camp previously and told Susan camp was great. Susan was completely unconvinced, but made a deal with her father that she would try it, knowing she could go and visit her sister if she lasted through the entire 10 days of camp.

Susan arrived at camp unexcited to say the least. She was extremely depressed. She spent most of the first day crying.

I tried talking with her, but she would not even look at me; she insisted on going home. She was angry, upset, and determined to leave.

I spent the first day doing my best to make camp enjoyable for her. Though Susan tried to sit by herself at meals, I continuously sat with her and encouraged her to come and join the rest of the team. When Susan refused to participate in conversation with other campers, I talked to some of our team members about approaching her. I was there as a friend to listen to her, and as a staff member to support her in staying.

At the end of the first day, Susan called her dad and begged to come home. However, her dad agreed with me that she should give camp a try for a little while. Susan continued to be angry and upset throughout the first two or three days. She was not easy to approach but I made her my challenge and committed myself to keeping her at camp and making it a positive experience. I tried joking with her, involving her, and just about everything I could think of to get her engaged in camp. There were definitely times I felt like she had made up her mind to leave, and times I felt all my efforts were not getting through. But I did not let Susan's negative attitude or insults deter me; I stayed committed to her.

Finally, I noticed Susan softening a little, which made my decision to stick with her a little easier. It was day four of camp and campers were sharing their experiences in front of the group when to my surprise, Susan raised her hand. Knowing the struggles Susan was having, the other staff members looked at me in disbelief. I was nervous, not knowing what she would say. Susan got up and stood in front of the 100 campers and 20-some staff. Tearfully, she began apologizing for her behavior for the past three days, "I apologize for my negative attitude, for not making camp *'This Is It,'* and for doubting the sincerity of everyone here. I know if I like camp this much on day four, I can't wait until day five!"

Listening to Susan, my eyes filled with tears. I was so proud of her! As she walked off the stage, everyone cheered. She did not want to be at camp, but she gave it a try and ended up loving it. I was so grateful that I had stayed committed to her. It was then that I realized just how rewarding the big challenges are in life.

After camp, Susan went to visit her sister who lived nearby. She lived near enough that Susan, who had at first hated camp, stopped by twice just to say, "Hi," and give me a great big hug.

Commit Yourself – And See What Happens
Bobbi DePorter

Becoming committed to something is really a two-step process: first you must discover your passion and then you must decide to follow it, no matter what.

Think about what excites you. What turns you on? What fires your passion? What prompts you to dream? What awakens your vision? Before creating the Burklyn Business School and SuperCamp, I had clear pictures in my mind of the possibilities these programs held. I could see, taste, hear, and feel those possibilities, and I felt driven to make them happen.

My partners and I were so excited by the idea of SuperCamp that it carried us through all the uncertainties, problems and crises of that first program. This excitement was infectious, spreading to others who became eager to send their children on this adventure to learning. At the end of the first SuperCamp, I saw children who had arrived shy and withdrawn stand before the entire group and loudly declare their pride in themselves. They told of their commitment to use their new skills and to live by the 8 Keys.

When I heard them, I was hooked. At that moment I thought, "This is what I am committed to; this is what my life is about – producing programs that support youth." That was 1982 and I am as committed to my vision today as I was on the final day of that first SuperCamp.

A "Win" for Everyone
Bobbi DePorter

Commitment can not only be tied to a principle, it can also produce satisfaction in bringing happiness to others. Back when I was at Hawthorne/Stone, one of our major projects was a condominium conversion of an apartment complex with 540 tenants, many of them retired. You can imagine how the tenants felt when we first visited the site after purchasing the property. I distinctly remember walking across the grounds while people stared at us skeptically from their windows. They were suspicious of us and worried about what would become of them and their homes.

But we were committed to making the conversion a "win" for everyone, so we started by talking privately with the tenants, getting to know them, and learning their dreams and desires. We talked publicly about our plans and even held open forums where we encouraged the tenants to ask questions. At the beginning of the process most of the tenants didn't even know each other and rarely smiled or spoke. By the end, we had happy, smiling tenants actually campaigning on our behalf. On their own initiative, they took city council members to lunch, telling them why they – the tenants – wanted the conversion. The council had never before approved a conversion and was reluctant to do so. If they had encountered any opposition from the tenants, they would have eagerly used it as an excuse to reject our proposal.

By listening to our tenants, we learned much about their desires, needs, and challenges. Many of them had dreamed for years of owning their own homes, yet felt they had no hope of making that dream a reality. Using various creative means, we were able to offer them the apartment/condos at special, affordable rates and terms. We also made arrangements for long-time tenants to continue to rent at reasonable rates. On the day of the hearing, the council chamber was standing-room-only with people spilling into the hallways. A steady stream of tenants testified on our behalf, and the conversion was approved.

I believe this happened because of our commitment to making it a win/win situation for everyone involved: the investors, the bank, our tenants, and ourselves. Many times we faced obstacles we thought were insurmountable. And we overcame them. Every new challenge was an opportunity to do whatever it took to accomplish our goal. We listened to the tenants' desires and structured the conversion to fill their needs as well as ours. We turned many tenants into happy homeowners, and made millions of dollars in the process. We kept our commitment to making people happy and improving their situation while making money for ourselves and our clients.

6

Ownership

Ownership

Take responsibility for actions

Be responsible for your thoughts, feelings,
words, and actions. "Own" the choices you make
and the results that follow.

When you live the Key of Ownership and take responsibility for the choices you make, your life changes. You have greater control because you stop blaming things outside yourself for your current situation. You can take ownership of your career, relationships, financial status, education, or other areas of your life. You can create a huge shift in your life simply by taking ownership of your attitude.

This was the case for Walter "Buddy" Davis, who contracted polio at age eight and was told he would never walk again. Under such circumstances, no one could have faulted him if he'd become depressed and withdrawn, denying he had a problem, or using the problem as an excuse for his lack of achievement.

But Buddy chose another approach. He took responsibility for his life and promised himself that not only would he walk again, but someday he would run. And did he ever! In fact, he won an Olympic gold medal and set a new world record for the high jump. Buddy took ownership of his attitude and it changed his life.

The Ownership Game

We can think of ownership as a game we play. On a blank piece of paper, draw a horizontal line across the center. Above the line, write the words Choices, Accountability, Freedom, Responsibility, Solutions, and Willingness. Below the line, write terms like Laying Blame, Justification, Denial, and Quitting.

There are two ways to play the game of ownership:
Playing above the line, and
Playing below the line

Playing above the line means taking responsibility, being accountable for your actions, and looking for solutions – in other words, taking ownership. Playing above the line leads to greater freedom, trust, and success. Rather than being controlled by circumstances, you determine your own actions.

Playing below the line means blaming others for your mistakes, justifying your actions, denying them, or just quitting before you reach your goal. You act as if circumstances are out of your control; it's not your fault and there's nothing you can do about it. Playing below the line is living in complacency and inaction. It's easy, but you don't get anywhere.

To be successful, play above the line. If you make a mistake, step up and take ownership of it. If you see something that needs to be done, take action and do it. Think of responsibility as "respond-ability." The ability to respond to what happens to you, rather than just accepting it. It takes action to make things happen.

Playing "Above the Line" —

Choices

Freedom

Accountability

Responsibility

Solutions

Willingness

Justification

Laying blame

Denial

Giving up

Reasons

— playing "Below the Line"

Ownership:
Taking responsibility
for your actions.

When you feel a sense

of ownership,

you take responsibility,

give your best effort,

and take pride

in the results.

Bridging the Gaps
David Evans

I stared down at my second high school progress report in utter disbelief. I truly could not believe they were my grades, someone must have made a mistake. I read down the list time and again, the letters burning into my eyes: D, B-, C-, C+, A-, D. Ever since grade school I had thought of myself as an "A student." I knew I was smart, and I hung out with the smart students. I even believed I deserved A's. Yet, in reality I was merely skating through school, hardly doing any work. Finally, after six years of avoiding the truth, it all came crashing down in my freshman year. Right then I stopped rationalizing my situation and made a conscious decision to change. I decided to get the A's that were locked up inside me. The rest of that year was spent laboriously developing study skills and habits to improve my grades. I decided to spend a week at SuperCamp, a motivational and skill-building camp held on the Stanford campus. My sophomore year I hit the ground running and received the first straight-A report card of my life. I never turned back. It was a great success, but it was also an awfully close call, nearly flushing my college aspirations down the tube.

If nothing else, my freshman year showed me the tremendous power of choice. Awareness of a material gap between our intention and our experience arrives as an attention-getting "aha," a "whack on the side of the head." If one can pin down the issue and accept the self-criticism offered by awareness, then the individual can begin to take ownership. The turning point comes as the individual makes the choice to accept the truth, to "own it." Once the problem is fully owned the decision must be made to take action, to do whatever it takes to succeed and "bridge the gap."

I hope others who are unaware of the gaps in their lives can learn to take charge of life. By taking ownership in our lives and exercising the tremendous power of choice, anything can be accomplished.

I'm living proof.

Ownership is the First Step Toward Success
Shelby Reeder
(Interview with Graham Silver)

Graham Silver had been saddled with a stuttering problem most of his life. His stuttering began when he was five years old. When he turned twelve, his stuttering changed to hesitation. As a child he was teased a lot, especially in junior high.

"Someone would ask me my name, just to get me going," Graham recalls. "I'd open my mouth to speak, but the words just wouldn't come out. Then they would say; hey, he doesn't even know his own name!"

By the eighth grade it got so bad he quit using his first name completely. He simply couldn't say it. He began going by his middle name, Richard.

His parents sent him to speech therapy programs, but nothing seemed to help. "I was in speech therapy for a long, long time. I would get comfortable there and after a while I would be able to talk fine. I'd think, great, I'm cured, but as soon as I walked out the door, it started again."

Today, Graham is a professional disc jockey. He is speaking in front of crowds every chance he gets. And he is good at it – so good that the company he worked for couldn't keep up with the requests for Graham to be a DJ at their parties. He now owns his own mobile DJ business, Silver Tunes. "It's funny," says Graham, "I used to be scared to talk to people I knew. Now I'm making cold calls."

How did Graham get from shy stutterer to wild and crazy DJ? "It didn't happen overnight," says Graham. He took ownership of his situation and began to build up confidence in himself, a little at a time.

Once he entered high school, things got a little better, but the real breakthrough came when he was a student at SuperCamp. Making new friends and completing the challenging ropes course improved his confidence. Eventually, he learned to speak up in front of his team. Then one night he got up the courage to speak in front of the entire camp.

"I was so overwhelmed, I burst into tears. It was the first time I really felt I didn't have to be afraid anymore."

After high school, Graham returned to SuperCamp as a staff member, and continued working faithfully for many summers. But the first staff training was another major breakthrough for Graham. He built up a lot of confidence and really opened up to people. "Suddenly, I found I could talk without stuttering. I was even able to say my first name again, for the first time in years. It felt great!"

Even today, Graham keeps pushing himself further, taking ownership for continued personal growth. He believes that if you push yourself a little at a time, eventually you'll reach your goal. "Don't expect it to happen overnight," he advises, "but if you keep that dream before you, eventually you can accomplish it."

Taking Ownership in Relationships
Ian Jackson

Clare and I always fought as kids, like a lot of brothers and sisters. She's three years older than I am, and as a true younger brother, I did my best to annoy her, especially with my innocent face telling my parents I did nothing wrong. I would complain about whatever she was doing or saying, all the time winding her up even more, only to watch her explode with fury at me. Then I would stand there looking shocked as if I had no idea where her anger came from. It was fun but it never really meant much, and I thought we'd grow up and everything would be fine between us.

As we got older, we started to respect each other more and get on better. We let each other be our own person a lot more. We each went our own ways – Clare travelling around the world and studying at university while I was still at high school, and I was working abroad and going to university when she finished. We each found our own lives. So much so, in fact, that we didn't really know each other anymore.

Clare became heavily involved in the church, and it became a big part of her life. Meanwhile, I went out with friends a lot. Any time Clare and I talked about the church, I felt sure she was trying to convert me, and I wanted to be in control of my own life, so I backed away more. We talked less, and any time she met up with me and my friends in a social atmosphere I felt very awkward – like I couldn't be myself with Clare there, and as if she was disapproving of my friends.

Gradually as we lived apart we saw each other less, and I made little effort to see her, thinking it would be awkward. I never called her – we mainly caught up on news through Mum and Dad.

I convinced myself that this was all okay, and that I was happy with the way it was. I told myself that we didn't have a bad relationship at all – after all, we never fought anymore. Any time Clare and I talked about not seeing each other, I would just say I was really busy and that she lived so far away that it was tough for me to see her. Any time it came up in conversation with my parents, I would blame Clare. It seemed that each of us thought the other was making no effort and that it was the other person's fault. Quite often I would just give up and say it was never going to change.

The moment I thought to myself that maybe I was part of the problem was the moment things *did* start to change.

When I spent time thinking about it, I realized I was half the relationship. I couldn't say it was all up to Clare and just wait for her to change. If I wanted change to happen, it had to start with me.

The more I thought about it, the more I realized that when we talked about church, Clare wasn't trying to convert me at all. It was, and is, a really large part of her life, and she wanted me to understand that. She wanted me to know more about who she was as a person. It was up to me how I wanted to interpret that, and I was just interpreting it in a way I didn't like. When I was becoming defensive about my friendships, and when I was feeling awkward around Clare, I was doing that to myself. Clare could never *make* me feel awkward or defensive – that was a choice only I could make. Eleanor Roosevelt said "No one can make you feel inferior without your consent" and as soon as I saw that quote, it really hit home with me. Clare doesn't control my emotions. I do. If I let anyone else control my emotions, I wouldn't be an individual. I'd be robbing myself of my own happiness, saying someone else controlled how I felt, as if someone else could also control my height, my weight, or my thoughts. It was *my* choice how I felt. So I decided to change how I felt around her. I've become receptive to hearing about what's going on in her life, and instead of feeling defensive and competitive, I can feel happy that things are going so well for her.

I decided to change my actions, too. Not making an effort was a choice, deliberate or not. I decided to make more

time for Clare, rather than fitting that time around everything else in my life. I have started to call her as much as
I'd call any other friend, and I've started listening to her. It
used to be that we would just talk to each other. Now we
listen to each other, too.

Now the relationship is starting to be not just something that
happened to me, but something that I am making happen.
And it's working for both of us. A friend told me, "it takes two
to tango, but it only takes one to make a difference," and he
was right. By my taking a step, we've both been more receptive to taking more steps.

Of course, it's not an overnight change, and we're not suddenly the closest brother and sister who ever lived, but it is
still a step in the right direction. We both know it's up to us.
That may seem like a small step, but for me that's huge.

Ownership Defines Personal Values
Rob Dunton

Ownership n. 1. The state of being an owner
2. Responsibility for one's actions

A little more than a month ago, I was in Tijuana, Mexico. I was returning from a night at the discos and was walking alone, back to the border. I passed a young child who had a small guitar in his lap and a cup with a few pesos in it. The child was sound asleep. I took out my wallet and placed a five-dollar bill in the cup, knowing full well that it would mean a tremendous amount to his livelihood. I walked on, an anonymous giver. The act was done, the impact made. A stadium of applauding onlookers wouldn't make the gift any more or less valuable.

Twenty years earlier, a friend of mine and I were wildly playing "air guitar" with my parents' guitars while they were out. In one frenzied heavy-metal move I cracked the neck on the guitar. It wasn't a highly visible break, but I could see the crack when I looked closely. I put the guitar back where I had found it and didn't say a word. No one else knew. The act was done, the impact made.

I wrongly assumed that if no one found out I broke the guitar, I was free of the responsibility for the damage I had caused. What I realize now is that nothing could change the fact that it was I who broke the guitar. The damage was done whether anybody found out or not, just as the value of the five dollars to the young street boy was the same whether or not he ever knew it was I who was bearer of the gift. My actions have results, good and bad, and I am the one responsible for them, whether or not anyone else ever knows what I did.

The principle of ownership starts with a clear understanding that we "own" the results of all our actions – no matter what. Hiding embarrassing acts or boasting of things that we wished we'd done doesn't affect the reality of our actions. Real acts of generosity, real honesty, real acts of courage or sympathy are the only things that count. Bogus displays of courage or generosity will last only as long as the appearance will, but more importantly, it's critical to understand that only *real* acts create *real* change.

And ownership is the start of it all.

Ownership Through Communication
Bobbi DePorter

We can take ownership of our lives every day, in many different ways. For example, we can demonstrate that we're taking ownership simply by the way we communicate. Recently, I was 20 minutes late for an important meeting on the other side of town. When I arrived, I could clearly see the person waiting for me was upset. I started to say, "I'm late because I got stuck in traffic," putting the blame on the traffic. Instead, I said, "I'm late because I got stuck in traffic. I knew there might be heavy traffic this time of day, and I should have left earlier. I'm sorry and I realize I cost you time waiting for me. Would you like me to stay later than we'd planned? Next time I'll leave earlier." Instantly, I saw the anger melt away from my associate's face. My taking ownership for the situation diffused his anger. It made him realize I was sincere in my apology.

It's Never Too Late
Marilyn Manning

Several years ago, while attending a communications course, I experienced a most unusual process. The instructor asked us to list anything in our past that we felt ashamed of, guilty about, regretted, or incomplete about. The next week he invited participants to read their lists aloud. This seemed like a very private process, but there's always some brave soul in the crowd who will volunteer. As people read their lists, mine grew longer. After three weeks, I had 101 items on my list. The instructor then suggested that we find ways to make amends, apologize to people, or take some action to right any wrongdoing. I was seriously wondering how this could ever improve my communications, having visions of alienating just about everyone in my life.

The next week, the man next to me raised his hand and volunteered this story: "While making my list, I remembered an incident from high school. I grew up in a small town in Iowa. There was a sheriff in town that none of us kids liked. One night, my two buddies and I decided to play a trick on Sheriff Brown. After drinking a few beers, we found a can of red paint, climbed the tall water tank in the middle of town, and wrote, on the tank, in bright red letters: Sheriff Brown is an s.o.b. The next day, the town arose to see our glorious sign. Within two hours, Sheriff Brown had my two pals and me in his office. My friends confessed and I lied, denying the truth. No one ever found out.

"Nearly 20 years later, Sheriff Brown's name appears on my list. I didn't even know if he was still alive. Last weekend, I dialed information in my hometown back in Iowa. Sure enough, there was a Roger Brown still listed. I dialed his number. After a few rings, I heard: 'Hello?' I said: 'Sheriff Brown?' Pause. 'Yup.' 'Well, this is Jimmy Calkins. And I want you to know that I did it.' Pause. 'I knew it!' he yelled back. We had a good laugh and a lively discussion. His closing words were: 'Jimmy, I always felt badly for you because your buddies got it off their chest, and I knew you were carrying it around all these years. I want to thank you for calling me...for your sake.'"

Jimmy inspired me to clear up all 101 items on my list. It took me almost two years, but became the springboard and true inspiration for my career as a conflict mediator. No matter how difficult the conflict, crisis, or situation, I always remember that it's never too late to clear up the past and begin resolution.

7

Flexibility

·

Flexibility

Be willing to do things differently

Recognize what's not working and be willing to change what you're doing to achieve your goal.

When you live the Key of Flexibility, you willingly adapt your thoughts and actions to changing or new situations. If you realize that what you're doing isn't working, you try something different until you find something that does work. Many times a day you're faced with situations that are different from what you had originally planned. One way to deal with these situations is to be rigid, or to continue to do things in the same way over and over; another is to handle them with flexibility.

One example of flexibility is the story of the chicken and the dog. Food was placed just beyond a fence. The chicken attempted to get the food by knocking its beak against the fence repeatedly until it was bloody. The dog also attempted to get the food, but when he realized that the fence was stopping him, he changed his strategy and went around the fence for the food. In our everyday situations, we need to look at our actions to see whether we are being rigid or flexible.

If a set of actions repeatedly fails to help us reach our goal, then it's time to change our strategy. Flexibility is a Key that reminds us to think about alternatives, leading us to new strategies – and ultimately to success.

In our own lives, it's not always so easy to recognize or admit when something isn't working. As a result, we sometimes find ourselves trying the same strategy over and over, even though it isn't producing the results we want. If this is true for you, you may be clinging to some ineffective beliefs. Perhaps someone told you it had to be done that way, or you believe there is only one right answer. Perhaps you've always done it that way, so why change?

The first step to using the Flexibility Key is to admit when something isn't working. Detach your ego from your actions and take an objective look at what you're doing. See your failure as a learning experience, use that valuable information to make adjustments and move on.

By exploring many possible solutions, you will discover avenues for success that you never would have considered previously. Perhaps you will even find ways to improve on things that are working, or fine-tune current systems or projects. By allowing yourself the freedom to investigate alternatives, you will eventually achieve the outcomes you desire. Life is fluid and changing, and options change, too. Seek out alternative routes and take charge of your situation.

Flexibility is being open to change and having the willingness to do things differently.

Be aware of the

possibility of a shift

in the way things

are usually done,

and be prepared to

take action.

Try Something Different
Unknown

I'm sitting in a quiet room at the Millcroft Inn, a peaceful little place hidden back among the pine trees about an hour out of Toronto. It's just past noon, late July, and I'm listening to the desperate sounds of a life-or-death struggle going on a few feet away. There's a small fly burning out the last of its short life's energies in a futile attempt to fly through the glass of the window. The whining wings tell the poignant story of the fly's strategy: Try Harder.

But it's not working.

The frenzied effort offers no hope for survival. Ironically, the struggle is part of the trap. It is impossible for the fly to try hard enough to succeed at breaking the glass. Nevertheless, this little insect has staked its life on reaching its goal through raw effort and determination.

This fly is doomed. It will die there on the windowsill. Across the room, twenty feet away, the door is open. Ten seconds of flying time and this small creature could reach the outside world it seeks. With only a fraction of the effort now being wasted, it could be free of this self-imposed trap. The breakthrough possibility is there. It would be so easy.

Why doesn't the fly try another approach, something dramatically different? How did it get so locked in on the idea that this particular route and determined effort offer the most promise for success? What logic is there in continuing until death to seek a breakthrough with more of the same?

No doubt this approach makes sense to the fly. Regrettably, it's an idea that will kill the fly.

Trying harder isn't always the solution to achieving more. It may not offer any real promise for getting what you want out of life. Sometimes, in fact, it's a big part of the problem. Stake your hopes for a breakthrough on trying harder than ever, and you may miss your chance for success. Try smarter. Not harder.

Choosing a Different Path
Ian Jackson

My goal at high school in England was always to graduate and get into a great university to study psychology. I applied to a university I really loved – the one that my sister had studied law at – and they offered me a place. I was really happy. Of course, it was dependent on me getting certain grades in my final high school exams. I had expected that – I was just happy to have the offer. I would just get the grades I needed and then go to work as an assistant teacher in a high school in Canada for a year before I started studying again.

It never occurred to me that I might not get the grades I needed. Ten days before my flight to Toronto, my exam results arrived. I needed three Bs. I got an A, a B – and a D!

I couldn't believe it. Hopefully they would still accept me. The D was in geography, after all. What do tectonic plates and glaciers have to do with how people's minds work?

I called the university straight away to ask, but my fears came true. They said they wouldn't take me. I was so upset. That was it, I thought. I'd have to cancel my trip to Canada and spend a year reading geography books again to get into a decent university, or rush into a decision about a university I didn't want to go to. I could still use the grades from my other subjects, and retake just that one class over the year, but I would need to go to another high school to do that. Suddenly everything that I'd been excited about seemed to be out of reach.

I thought it was safest to stay home and work, instead of going to Canada. That thought stuck in my head. It was the safest thing to do.

Safest. Most comfortable.

The more I thought about that the more it bothered me. I knew I had so much to offer, but that wasn't going to come out of me if I was too busy being comfortable.

My parents and family supported me completely in my decision to go to Canada. They helped me out the whole time I was there, sending me information about universities in Britain, giving me encouragement, and helping me find different ways of looking at the situation. This was all about finding different ways to reach my goals, they told me.

I had an amazing time in Canada, and I completely changed from how I'd been in high school. I became independent, responsible, mature, and someone that people looked up to. I often joke to friends about August 31st, 1995, being the day my life really began, but it's something that is really true to me in so many ways. During a vacation, I flew back to Britain, and looked at various universities in England and Scotland. I decided to apply again. Without even being asked for one interview, I was given unconditional offers of university places from seven of the eight universities I applied to.

They each told me that working abroad was impressive, and had helped me get the place. Getting into a good university wasn't all about studying and getting good grades, they told me. It was about experience. By now I had a lot of great experience.

In the week before I left for Canada and the start of the rest of my life, I had been stuck thinking that I was doing the wrong thing in going abroad. I had been stuck in the paradigm of studying. I saw my goal and thought I knew how to get there. I wasn't taking a step back and looking at what I was doing.

If I had taken a step back at the time, I would have seen what I see now – that there are several different paths to a goal. I saw only one and nearly limited myself. Fortunately I realized there was another path, one that opened up the rest of my life. Letting go of the old path and going down a new one took a lot of courage, and it was the best decision of my life.

Discovering Opportunities
Mike Hernacki

Richard, a carpenter and high school dropout, considered himself poor at "book learning." But as he got older, he found it too physically taxing to do carpentry. The trouble was, there were no other jobs available in his field and he was facing the prospect of a permanent layoff.

He then discovered he could learn engineering using the same techniques he used to learn carpentry – not by reading and writing, but by using his hands to make models, sketching his ideas on paper, and talking about them with his instructors. He employed his old learning styles to a new situation.

In this way, he was able to learn enough to become a junior engineer in his 50s and go to work for an aerospace firm. When the aerospace firm lost a number of big defense contracts and laid Richard off, he was again able to translate what he knew to a different field – this time, shipbuilding. Last I heard, he was supervising a team of workers who do with steel what carpenters do with wood.

Circumventing Obstacles with Flexibility
Michelle Vyvjala

Flexibility is the willingness to change what we are doing to achieve the outcome desired. Flexibility allows us to choose the best option to accomplish the outcome. With that said, flexibility to me is when you go around an obstacle course to get to your goal. In other words, when something or someone gets in your way, you can still find a way to reach your goal. If you are not flexible, you will become part of the problem, not the solution.

I showed flexibility recently when I broke my ankle. I had to take two weeks off from school in order to let the swelling in my ankle go down. With finals only a month away, I had to really keep on the ball with my schoolwork. I had so much make-up work to do that I often had to stay up really late and study. I was pushing myself harder and longer than my friends. I was not expecting to have this much work, so I had to be flexible and get help. I was sometimes unable to go out on weekends, and during Christmas break I had to spend my time working on school assignments instead of relaxing with my friends. It took a lot of commitment on my part, but it was worth it. I only achieved my goal by using understanding and flexibility. My willingness to change my schedule and myself helped me reach my goals. Because I took that extra step, focused on the goal, not the problem, and stuck to it, I can now be proud of myself.

The Babysitting Job
Ryan Day

There is always more than one way to solve any situation that presents itself. It is just a matter of looking at the various options that are available. It takes looking around and keeping your mind open to all suggestions that are offered.

At the age of ten I thought I was responsible enough to baby-sit younger children, and could not understand why the mothers in the neighborhood did not hire me. I would always offer to watch their children, and they would always say they would keep me in mind. I waited for the call, but the phone never rang.

I figured I needed a new approach; instead of asking if I could babysit while the parents were out, I began to ask if I could come over and entertain the children while the parents were home. I offered to take the children for walks around the neighborhood and to the park to play.

The mothers agreed, and watched me as I cared for their children. Then one day when I was at one of the neighborhood homes the mother needed to run to the store. I offered to take her child to my house, where my mom was home, and watch her child there. To my surprise, she said yes! I was thrilled.

As time passed and I got older, more mature and responsible, parents became more trusting of me with their children. I was eventually babysitting on my own just like I had wanted. Once I used new strategies to start babysitting, the rest fell into place.

Success Comes in Many Different Ways
Bobbi DePorter

Recently, I found it necessary to visit one of our SuperCamp program sites. Two key staff members, Jeff and Karen, weren't getting along and it was affecting our entire program. Both of them felt "right" in their assessment of the situation. Four of us sat down to discuss the predicament: a counselor, Jeff and Karen, and myself. It soon became clear that no matter how long we talked, the situation would not be resolved.

The situation called for flexibility. Karen decided to take an early transfer to another program where she was scheduled to be in the future.

This seemed like a positive solution to the problem because: The current program would run easier (as Jeff said, "easier, not better") because the personalities involved would be different; and Karen could go to her other program in time for the training, which would increase her success there.

In spite of the advantages of this solution, both Karen and Jeff felt a sense of loss. I watched them both struggle with the decision. They each believed they'd let me down by being unable to work together successfully. But not everyone is meant to work together easily and I didn't look at this situation as a failure. I simply saw it as a time for flexibility, a time to search for a solution that had positive advantages. The key, which isn't always so easy, is to let go of the emotional feelings of not being successful in a particular way and accept being successful in a different way.

William's Story
Bobbi DePorter

Back when I was working for a real estate and investment company, I had a friend and co-worker who was at one time the antithesis of flexibility. Of course, William had his good points – he was a nice person and a hard worker, highly organized, and would do anything to support the company. But he was also rigid, reserved, and meticulous. He was obsessive with his files and record-keeping, and sometimes got upset if we touched anything on his desk. Everything in his world was neat, orderly, and planned in advance. He always followed the rules and had a strong need to always be "right." He was a very serious person, rarely joining us for dinner or a movie. William didn't do things for fun – "a waste of time," he grumbled.

Then seemingly overnight, William showed up at work a different person. There was a sudden shift in his personality. He was pleasant to be around, open, and friendly. He laughed and had fun and enjoyed other people's company. As days passed, he became very active socially, inviting us to join him for lunch or dinner, movies, tennis, or skiing. "Let's go out after work!" became his favorite refrain. He became spontaneous and carefree.

William began taking the time to call people and have long conversations. He expressed his thoughts and feelings, and listened to others' problems and concerns. Soon, he was a caring ear for all who knew him.

He also began to travel – without plan or itinerary, just taking off for months and going where he chose. He was very unlike his old self.

Everyone was amazed with the changes he had made in his life. "William is a model of positive attitude and living!" we commented. He was lighthearted and a joy to be with. People wanted to emulate him and just hang out with him. This went on for about six months.

And then one day, without any warning, the news came. William had killed himself.

True to his previous nature, William had taken care of everything. His finances and papers were in order. His home was neat and organized. Beforehand, William had even called the coroner and told him to come and pick up his body. He left a note behind for all his friends. "I must go," it read. "I had planned this six months ago...I do care for you all."

We all gathered together, trying to make sense of this tragedy. How could we not have picked up on the signals? What could we have done to be there for him, as he had been there for us over the last few months? Even on the very morning of his death, William had played tennis with a friend, laughing, and enjoying himself. What had gone wrong?

We talked for hours asking, "What can we learn from this?" One lesson we learned from how William lived his life was Flexibility. When he made the decision to end his life, William changed from rigid and inflexible to spontaneous and caring. He made many changes in his life. But, in a way, his rigidity was still a part of him. Once he had made his decision to kill himself, he was compelled to follow through. He could not change his plan.

In his last days, William's life was a model of how to live. How many of us still live like the old William, inflexible in the way we do things and afraid to change, or afraid to show others that we care? Although his life ended too soon, I admire William's courage, if even for just a short time. He had always been reserved and unsociable; suddenly he was reaching out to others. His life had been rigid and carefully planned – yet he learned to be spontaneous and carefree. It took courage to make the changes that he made, even if they only lasted a little while.

To this day, I cannot understand how William could live his life in such a positive, joyful manner, yet choose to end it. Once he applied Flexibility, he discovered so much and grew so much as a person. But from him we can still learn to live fully by modeling the positive aspects of his life without the harsh decision that he made at the end. Make the commitment to be positive, flexible, caring, and joyful, making the most of each day of your life.

8

Balance

Balance

Live your best life

Be mindful of self and others while focusing on what's
meaningful and important in your life. Inner happiness and
fulfillment come when your mind, body, and emotions
are nurtured by the choices you make.

Balance enables you to live your best life. Making choices
that nurture your mind, body and emotions brings a feeling
of wellbeing ... you are happy, healthy, and productive.
When you're in balance, you make time for the things that
are meaningful and important for you in every area of your
life: school, work, hobbies, family, friends, health, and self.
You may be busy, but balance helps you make time for it all.
Consequently, you are more fulfilled because you are
engaged in the things that really matter to you.

Staying in balance is an ongoing process. As we move
through our lives each day, we make thousands of adjustments in thought, behavior, and feelings. We adjust to our
surroundings, the people we encounter, and our physical
requirements. When questions arise about how we spend our
time, we make choices depending on what's important in the
moment. We may have to forego time with friends to meet
commitments at work, or leave work to care for a sick child.
We make adjustments along the way to stay positively
aligned with our world.

Balance is a subtle Key. It brings a quiet peace that is not always obvious. However, when we're out of balance we know it. Stress, exhaustion, illness, anger, depression, or just feeling tired or irritated are all signs of being out of balance. When imbalance strikes, take a moment to reflect on what areas you may be ignoring, then take action. Sometimes getting in balance calls for long-term measures like changing your diet and joining a health club. Other times, simply taking a walk or visiting a friend will do the trick. Whatever it is, once you have achieved balance, you'll feel better.

To stay in balance, check in with yourself daily. Ask yourself, "What do I value? What's really meaningful and important to me? Does this need to be done right now? What is the priority?" These simple questions help you focus on the things that are most important to you. When you have extra demands to meet and you feel your stress level rising, take time to prioritize your activities, making sure to leave time for yourself.

Be aware that you may not achieve perfect balance every day. Things come up that demand extra attention – deadlines for projects or studying for exams – and while you're putting extra energy and time into these areas to assure your success, you may have to ignore other activities, like going to the gym. During these times, be aware of the choice you're making and commit to getting back in balance once the project is completed. There may always be things you have to say "No" to, but making those choices gets easier if you keep the "big picture" of your life before you and become more aware of what you need to do to stay in balance.

When life appears too complicated and demanding, the Key of Balance refocuses our attention on the things we value and keeps us moving forward. We know the peacefulness of being in balance when we nurture our minds, bodies, and emotions.

Balance is an ongoing process demanding continual adjustments.

You may need to check in with yourself daily and ask:

What do I value?

::

What's really important to me?

The Ride for Life
Mindy Hurt

"Today, you embark on a four-day journey." The voice echoed through the Houston Astrodome marking the beginning of a charity bike ride which would take me 350 miles from Houston to Dallas.

"There will be good times. There will be difficult times. There will be times when you want to quit," the voice continued.

"Know that whatever happens, in four days it will be over. Whatever you achieve, whatever you accomplish, what you will remember the most are the people you meet along the way. Don't get so focused on the accomplishment that you forget to see the people."

The words continue to challenge and guide me. They taught me a lesson I wasn't expecting: a lesson in BALANCE.

When I signed up for Tanqueray's Texas AIDS Ride 2, I had three personal objectives:
- To stretch my limits and reach beyond the excuses that keep life ordinary.
- To strengthen my relationship with my sister who was also my riding and fundraising partner in the event.
- To see how I honored the key of Commitment in my life. How far was I willing to go to help someone I've never met?

"Whatever you think this journey is going to be, you will be wrong," I heard across the speakers. "Expect the unexpected."

And so it began.

We rode out of downtown Houston at dawn with a police escort. Everywhere I looked, extraordinary people surrounded us. There were people lined up in the streets holding signs of thanks. People honked their horns in encouragement. School children waved from the schoolyard steps as 615 cyclists pedaled slowly down their street. We rode and rode and rode.

Ninety miles and 9 hours later, my sister Laura and I arrived at camp. That's when the "real" journey began.

Laura wasn't feeling well when we arrived, so we took her to the medical tent. Assuming she just needed a little rest,

I showered and set up our tent. But she wasn't feeling better. In fact, she was getting worse. We decided it would be best if she slept in the Med Tent that night. She wouldn't be riding Day Two.

I went to bed to be ready for the next day. Around midnight, a flashlight was shined into my tent. "We've called an ambulance for your sister," a voice said. "She had a seizure and we're taking her to the emergency room as a precaution."

I found myself in a dilemma. I made a commitment to give my all to the ride. People had given money on my behalf. I knew that going to the emergency room would mean I wouldn't complete the ride on Day Two. And yet, the thought was fleeting. My sister was probably scared and confused. I had a commitment to her, too.

A voice in my head reminded me, "Don't get so focused on the *accomplishment* that you forget about *the people.*"

That's when I discovered the power of the Key of Balance. It's about remembering priorities, putting them in order, and having faith that there will be a way to fulfill all of our commitments.

So I shifted the focus of my journey and chose to put my sister first. I chose the journey that took me from the emergency room of a small rural clinic to the Intensive Care Unit at a major hospital. I slept in waiting rooms, made difficult phone calls to family and friends, and spent the next 48 hours living from visiting hour to visiting hour as Laura recovered.

I saw firsthand the effects of a body being out of balance. Laura suffered from "water intoxication," an unusual condition caused by excessive water (she drank more than five gallons in eight hours) and not enough Gatorade to replenish the electrolytes, sodium, and potassium she lost during the ride.

The effect of her imbalance was completely debilitating. She was incoherent and aggressive. She didn't recognize or respond to anyone. For two days, doctors slowly restored her system. It took another week for her to fully regain mental clarity. She doesn't remember any of it.

After Laura was released from the hospital, I caught up with the riders about 100 miles outside of Dallas. As we rode united toward downtown Dallas, I became very aware of how extraordinary our body can be when it is in balance. These people rode 350 miles though heat and through sleet (we had both!), up hills, and against driving winds all based on a commitment to help people in need.

I realized the magnitude of the power I could have by keeping my life more in balance. Instead of getting absorbed in my work and all the things I have to do, I now remember to take time to enjoy myself, to connect with family and friends, and to feed my soul with beauty and nature.

Today, I'm proud of my accomplishments. And yet, the memories I treasure most are of the people I meet along the way. By keeping things in balance, there's plenty of room for both.

·

Balance is the Key to an Active Live
Ian Jackson

My first three years at university were fun. When I wasn't studying, I was out with friends and meeting new people. Whenever people asked me what I liked to do in my spare time, I always talked about travelling around the world, which I did in my vacations. If people asked me about what I did in my spare time at university though, I couldn't think of much to say. I told them I didn't have the time to do much, because of my schoolwork. A lot of the time I even convinced myself that I didn't have the time to do anything else but study, especially while I was sitting in front of the TV. Everyone else I saw seemed to be doing stuff all the time, and even though I was getting good grades, I knew there was something missing.

After my first summer at SuperCamp, I realized what that was – it was balance. Balance didn't mean spending my time going between studying, friends, and the TV. It meant so much more. It meant looking after my mind, my body, and my spirit. I started going to the gym more, and noticed that although I found it hard going at first, the more exercise I did, the more I enjoyed it and the better I felt about myself as a person. This showed up in my grades. Then I started to work as the Public Relations Officer for the university's student travel agency. Suddenly something that seemed like it would take up too much time seemed to give me more time. I was organizing my time more, and creating opportunities for myself that I had never had before, giving presentations to hundreds of people, organizing events, meeting a lot of new friends, and appearing on an international TV chat-show!!!

Entering my final year at university, I started to realize how much there was that I was interested in. I realized that I had enough time for every area of my life if that was what I really wanted. With my goal that I had created at SuperCamp ("No wasted time") up on my wall, I started to become involved in more and more different things. The travel agency asked me back for a second year, and I also applied to work for the student counselling service nightline (something I wanted to do years ago, but convinced myself I didn't have enough time). I started learning a new recipe to cook for myself almost every night. I started a website for my friends from around the world to use to keep in touch with each other. I will soon be taking guitar lessons (another life-long goal). I've started to go to church, and I still go to the gym, and write in my journal. And my travels this year have included hiking around Europe, camping in Yosemite National Park, working in California, and trips to New England, Florida, and Ireland. And I still manage to spend more time with my family than I did during my first three years at university. From time to time I still watch TV too. And I'm enjoying my schoolwork more now than ever before.

I have been told that despite all my interests, I seem to be doing very well in each of them. It's not *despite* my interests, though. It's *because* of them.

The success I experience in one area of my life spills over into the other areas. And I'm learning to be more successful every single day.

The Game of Life
Christy McConnell

In the game of life, I choose to be a player, not a spectator. I choose to return, I choose to win. I want to thrive in sportsmanship rather than competition, teamwork rather than separation. You see, in life, we all are a team. We must work together, cooperate together, and win *together*. Our strategy for life may be simple, yet so brilliant that success is inevitable.

Let our captain be Love. Let love lead us to ecstasy and bond us together. Let our coach be Integrity. Let it teach us respect, kindness, honesty. Let the referee be Compassion, for without understanding we cannot communicate. Without each member of our precious team, the game is over before the whistle is even blown.

.

Variety Keeps Life in Balance
Shelby Reeder
(Interview with Luke Johnson)

SuperCamp grad Luke Johnson is one of those people who approaches something new by jumping right in. At age eighteen, he has already immersed himself in a wide variety of academic disciplines and life experiences. His interests include psychology, philosophy, sociology, evolution, and writing.

"The wider your knowledge base, the deeper your appreciation of all subjects," Luke says. "All areas are really interconnected in some way. The more you learn, the more you see the connections."

Luke's latest passion is film. To learn more about film-making, he spent last summer in Mexico on a film crew for a new television series. Characteristically, he did a little bit of everything.

"I worked as a second assistant to the director. I broke down the script, made schedules, and assisted in other ways. I also worked on the sound recording, I was a stunt man, and I was an actor in one episode."

Working on a film crew may sound glamorous, but it was also hard work. Luke worked 14 hours a day, six days a week. At the time, he was also writing a book and exercising two hours a day. "I did more than I ever thought I could," he says. "After that, school was comparatively easy."

Luke had been struggling in school, due to a lack of interest in his classes. "I'd tend to fall asleep in class," he admits. His experience on the film crew and a switch to a more challenging private school helped Luke get his life back in balance. He managed to raise his grades and is now considering attending college at either the University of Southern California or New York University. He plans to double major in psychology and film, then go to law school. He intends to make money in the field of law, then take time to write a book or direct a film.

Luke believes in expanding his skills and knowledge in as many directions as he can. "Don't nail yourself down to one thing," he advises. "The straight path limits what you see of life. It's important to know what's wrong with the wrong path as well as what's right with the right path."

Throughout life, he will continue his search for knowledge and new experiences. "Every step I take, I try to take a step away from what I've done before."

When you live the Key of Balance, you are at your most efficient level. It is amazing all the things you can accomplish. So whether you like to jump right into something or first test the waters, go ahead and take that first step. It's the only way to grow.

Achieving Balance in Mind, Body, and Emotions
Shelby Reeder
(Interview with Rachel Kochackis)

For those of you who are wondering just how long these SuperCamp skills and 8 Keys lessons really last, listen carefully. This is Rachel Kochackis' story...

Way back in 1983, Rachel's parents shipped her off to SuperCamp in Alta, Utah. This was only the second SuperCamp program, ever. SuperCamp was a new idea back then, and TV cameras, radio stations, and newspapers were covering the event. The fledgling program taught Rachel a lot about learning-to-learn skills, confidence building and the 8 Keys. Her parents liked the program so much they sent her to SuperCamp again in 1985. This time she found things were much different – there were many more students and new activities, including an intimidating ropes course.

Rachel found the ropes course, which demanded physical activity and agility, extremely challenging. "I was a hundred pounds overweight," she recalls. "Of all the things at SuperCamp this was definitely the most difficult."

The event dubbed "the pole" – a 60-foot climb up a pole or tree culminating in a breathtaking jump to a trapeze – is the event she remembers most vividly.

"I remember the climb was more of a challenge than any-thing else. Once I was up there, I convinced myself to jump no matter what my mind told me. The repelling, the tight rope, all these things were secondary challenges to me because I was not in good enough physical shape to climb that tree very easily. The two-by-fours nailed to the tree for a ladder were not an easy access for 5'1", 200-pound me."

Once she did it, she felt invincible. Now, many years later, she still recalls that feeling – the exhilaration, the excitement, the cheering crowd. It gives her a mental boost whenever she is faced with a challenge in her life.

However, the thing that made the biggest difference for Rachel was the introduction to a new way of thinking – learning to say, "I can" instead of "I can't."

"I learned so much about how the mind can affect everything – that if you tell yourself, 'I can,' you at least have a chance of reaching your goal. If you tell yourself, 'I can't' then you are defeated before you even begin."

Rachel says it took her a long time to realize the power of this simple philosophy and to get her life in balance.

"Well over 12 years later, everything I learned at SuperCamp had sunk in. I began a journey of a thousand miles. In eight months I lost 80 pounds and became a certified personal trainer. I found myself repeating a lot of what I learned at SuperCamp to my clients, as well as to the people in the crisis home where I volunteered. I am now a graphic designer. SuperCamp and the 8 Keys planted the seeds that have helped me become successful today."

Making a Choice
Bobbi DePorter

As president of my own company, my life is a busy one. And, like most people, I sometimes feel like I am being pulled in several directions at once. Family, friends, career, and colleagues all stake their claim on my time. Using the Key of Balance, I find that I can keep my priorities before me and make choices I can feel good about.

My top priorities are always my family and my work. I hold these two areas above all other commitments. However, commitments to work and family are sometimes in conflict, calling for some tough decision making. A recent family function

– my nephew's wedding – is a case in point. It was expected to be a large affair, with relatives flying in from all over the country. I planned to go, and was looking forward to it, when I received an unexpected invitation to China. I was to speak on education and SuperCamp in front of hundreds of people. It would further our understanding about education, and possibly even lay the groundwork for future SuperCamp programs in that country. It was an unusual opportunity I felt would not come again. It happened to be at the same time as the wedding.

Family members wanted me to attend the wedding, and at the time I felt pulled toward the wedding as much as the trip. It was a difficult decision, and I chose China. My family was disappointed and I felt I was letting them down. However, I am excited about our work and opportunities to further our vision of improving education worldwide. It is something I am committed to making happen. It was a choice I made.

To stay in Balance, understand the choices you make. What do you say "yes" or "no" to? Where do you draw your line in the sand, defining the things you are committed to and refusing others? Because life presents so many opportunities, there will be conflicts, a feeling of being pulled in too many directions at once. Knowing what your priorities are helps you make the tough decisions and stick with your vision – the big picture.

Overdoing It

Sometimes it's not a matter of choosing between two options; it's a matter of choosing to do too much. In one busy month, I attended a conference held by the American Camping Association, attended our own staff training seminar, and went on a business trip to Jakarta. In the midst of this hectic schedule, I also had the opportunity to spend a week with family at Walt Disney World. Of course, I went. Time with my children and grandchildren is something I value highly, so how could I say no?

It was well worth it. I saw my grandchildren take their first swim strokes, enjoyed the park and spent time with my family. But it was hardly a relaxing trip, getting up early each morning and getting in late each night. After traveling for nearly a month, I felt extremely out of balance.

Once I got home, I took some much-needed "down time" to gather my thoughts. I enrolled in an eight-week exercise program. And, strangely enough, I started cleaning everything! Closets, cabinets, desks, file drawers – nothing was safe from my urge to clean. In looking back, I think that I needed that time to get grounded, putting things back in order in my surroundings as well as my body and my mind.

Every moment of every day, we are making choices about how we spend our time. By being aware of our priorities, we can choose to spend time in ways that support these priorities and fulfill our commitment to our vision.

Tying Them All Together

- *Keys of Success*   Aaron White
- *Balancing the 8 Keys*   Ryan Day

Keys of Success
Aaron White, age 13

If I crumble under pressure
Or I let the whole stack drop,
If Failure never Leads to Success,
Will my Commitment stop?

If I don't have Flexibility,
And I just don't react,
If my decisions aren't right,
Will I still bounce back?

If I lose my Balance,
And suddenly I trip,
If the whole master plan fails,
Will I take Ownership?

If I don't use Integrity,
Will I lose people's trust?
If I don't Speak With Good Purpose,
Will my success rust?

I've learned about the skills of life,
I must get up and go!
If I don't make it This Is It,
I may stop the show.

I cannot fail. I must succeed.
I've been through this before.
I have the power of eight Keys,
And I've unlocked the door.

Balancing the 8 Keys
Ryan Day

The 8 Keys of Excellence are my life. Every Key flows into the other to support me every day in living the fullest life possible. My Failure Leads to Success: when I fail, I look for the learning and remain Committed to the goal. When the first attempt doesn't work, I become Flexible. I change direction and move forward. Giving up is not an option — I am too Committed. My actions and behaviors are mine to Own. When they are on target I feel proud and when I miss the mark I acknowledge that and try something different. I Speak with Good Purpose, I think about the words I say and how they will be heard, understood, and interpreted. Is my communication open, honest, direct, and clear? I remember, as I am going through my day, that my attitude affects my results. This Is It, after all — I'll never have this time again — am I making the best use of my time, energy, and efforts? The Keys have become my values and my behaviors demonstrate them. When I follow the 8 Keys of Excellence I have Integrity, Balance, and joy.

8 Keys of Excellence

Remember to...

Live in INTEGRITY

Acknowledge FAILURE LEADS TO SUCCESS

SPEAK WITH GOOD PURPOSE

Live in the Now – THIS iS IT!

Affirm your COMMITMENT

Take OWNERSHIP

Stay FLEXIBLE

Keep Your BALANCE

Since 1981, Quantum Learning Network (QLN) has produced educational programs for students, educators and business. Its vision is to create a shift in how people learn, so that learning will be joyful, challenging, engaging and meaningful.

Programs and products of QLN —

Quantum Learning Programs

Quantum Learning is a comprehensive model of effective learning and teaching. Its programs include: **Quantum Learning for Teachers**, professional development programs for educators providing a proven, research-based approach to the design and delivery of curriculum and the teaching of learning and life skills; **Quantum Learning for Administrators**, programs for enhancing leadership skills, productive team building, keeping teachers resourceful, and establishing a positive, productive atmosphere; **Quantum Learning for Students,** programs that help students master powerful learning and life skills; and **Quantum Learning for Business,** working with companies and organizations to shift training and cultural environments to ones that are both nurturing and effective.

SuperCamp

The most innovative and unique program of its kind, SuperCamp incorporates proven, leading-edge learning methods that help students succeed through the mastery of academic, social and everyday life skills. Programs are held across the U.S. on college campuses, as well as internationally, for three age levels: Junior Forum (11-13), Senior Forum (14-18), and Quantum U (18-24).

QLN Products

Quantum Learning Network offers a variety of books, DVDs, videos, CDs, and other products that support effective learning and teaching. All are based on our Quantum Learning methods, the "secret ingredient" for joyful, engaging, and meaningful learning. Developed over more than 25 years of SuperCamp and teacher-training experience, Quantum Learning continues to bring significant "shifts" for students, teachers, parents, and business people. Visit www.QLN.com to view the complete line of products.

QLN⊘ quantum learning network®

1938 Avenida del Oro, Oceanside, CA 92056
760-722-0072 • 800-285-3276 • Fax 760-305-7766
email: info@QLN.com • www.QLN.com

8 Keys of Excellence
Making Great Kids Greater

The Excellence Effect is a movement to inspire character, confidence, motivation, and leadership among today's youth through the 8 Keys of Excellence Family Program and the 8 Keys of Excellence School Program.

A significant long-term study found that the only two direct links to increasing positive behavior and preventing bad behavior in our youth are relationship with one's family and connectedness to school. The Excellence Effect movement builds both.

Through the 8 Keys of Excellence Family and School Programs, the Excellence Effect inspires individuals to internalize positive guiding principles that become their "core." We all operate from a core that's created from our environment. When we consciously create a positive core, a core that guides our decisions and actions, it transforms our lives ... and causes an effect on others ... who cause an effect on even more people.

> *The goal of the Excellence Effect is to transform the lives of 50 million young people by the year 2015. When this critical mass is achieved a shift will take place. Youth will believe in themselves, have the character and confidence to speak up and be proud of who they are, and create a positive future of inspired global citizens.*

The 8 Keys of Excellence Family Program is a transformational experience that builds communication, character and inspiration. The online program includes guidance for engaging conversations and fun activities that deepen the family relationship.

The 8 Keys of Excellence School Program is a year-long character development program for K-12 schools that inspires students to make positive choices about how they live their lives and become productive members of their schools, their families, and their communities. The online curriculum includes training videos, lessons, student journals and much more.

The 8 Keys of Excellence Family and School Programs are initiatives of Learning Forum International, a 501(c)(3) non-profit educational organization.

www.8Keys.org

Bobbi DePorter has changed the lives of over four million kids through her SuperCamp and Quantum Learning school programs. Author of over a dozen books, she is acknowledged by many as a leading authority on effective learning and youth development.

Bobbi broke the mold in the early eighties by creating a learning and life skills academic summer program for youth. Not your traditional camp and far from school, SuperCamp created an innovative category in engaged, joyful, successful learning. Now with more than 50,000 graduates and programs in the U.S., Europe, Asia and Latin America, SuperCamp is an established leader in the field of youth development.

The success of SuperCamp led Bobbi to create Quantum Learning school programs for educators and students. Quantum Learning is now a comprehensive school reform model producing significant positive change in thousands of schools and districts across the nation.

Bobbi is Chairman and President of Quantum Learning Network, founded in 1982. She has a rich history in effective learning and teaching. Bobbi studied with the renowned Bulgarian educator Dr. Georgi Lozanov in the late 1970s and was an early pioneer of accelerated learning in the United States. She is a past president of the International Alliance for Learning, its leading association.